Beautiful Large Print Simple Flowers

This Coloring book belongs to:

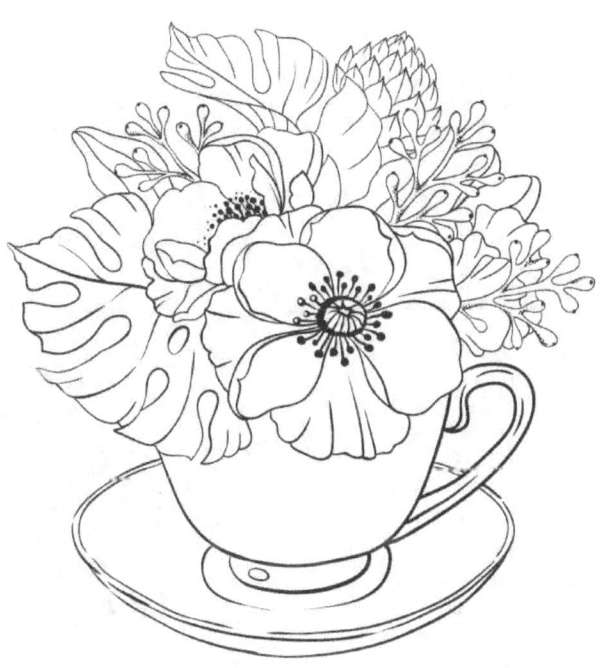

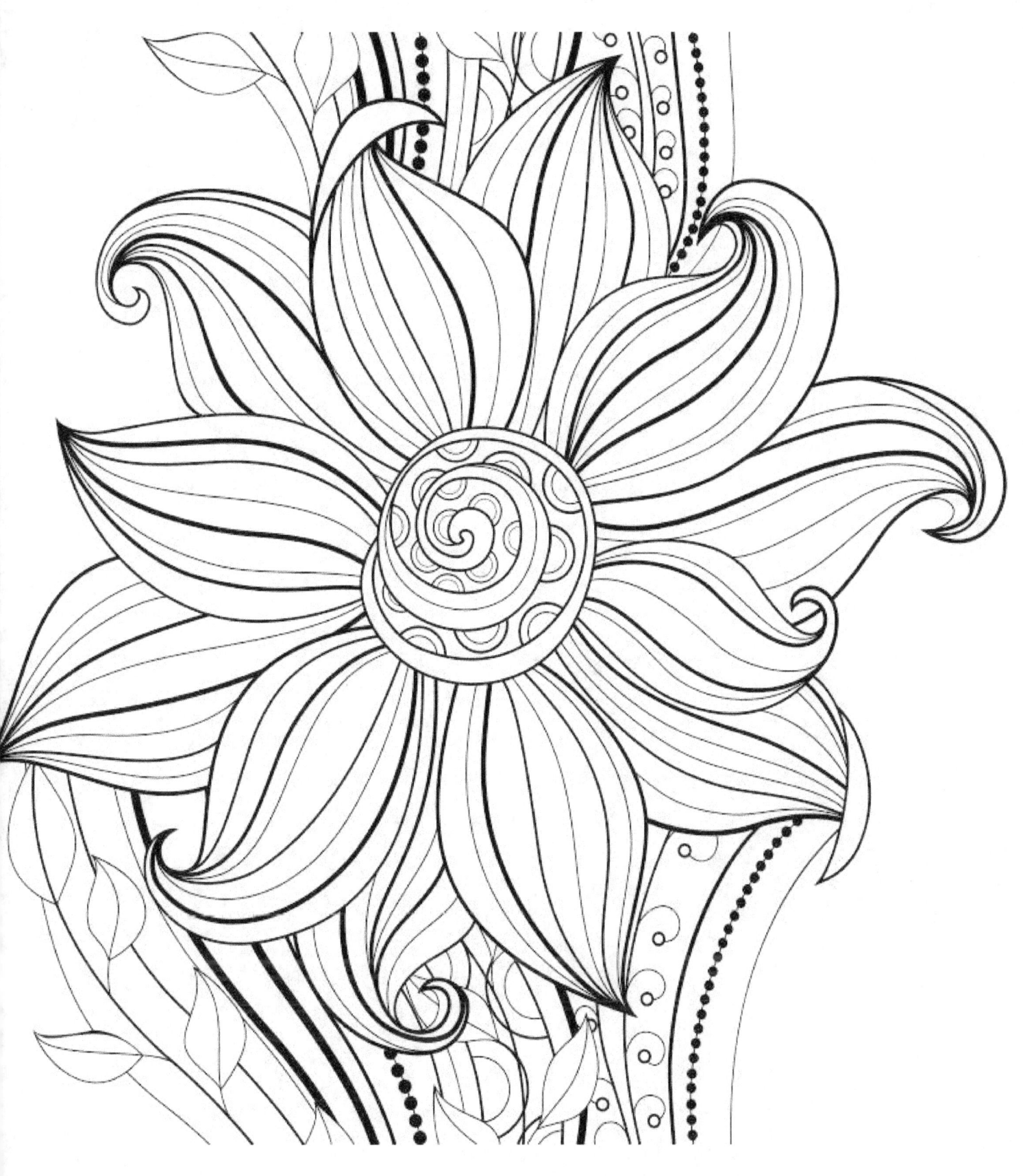

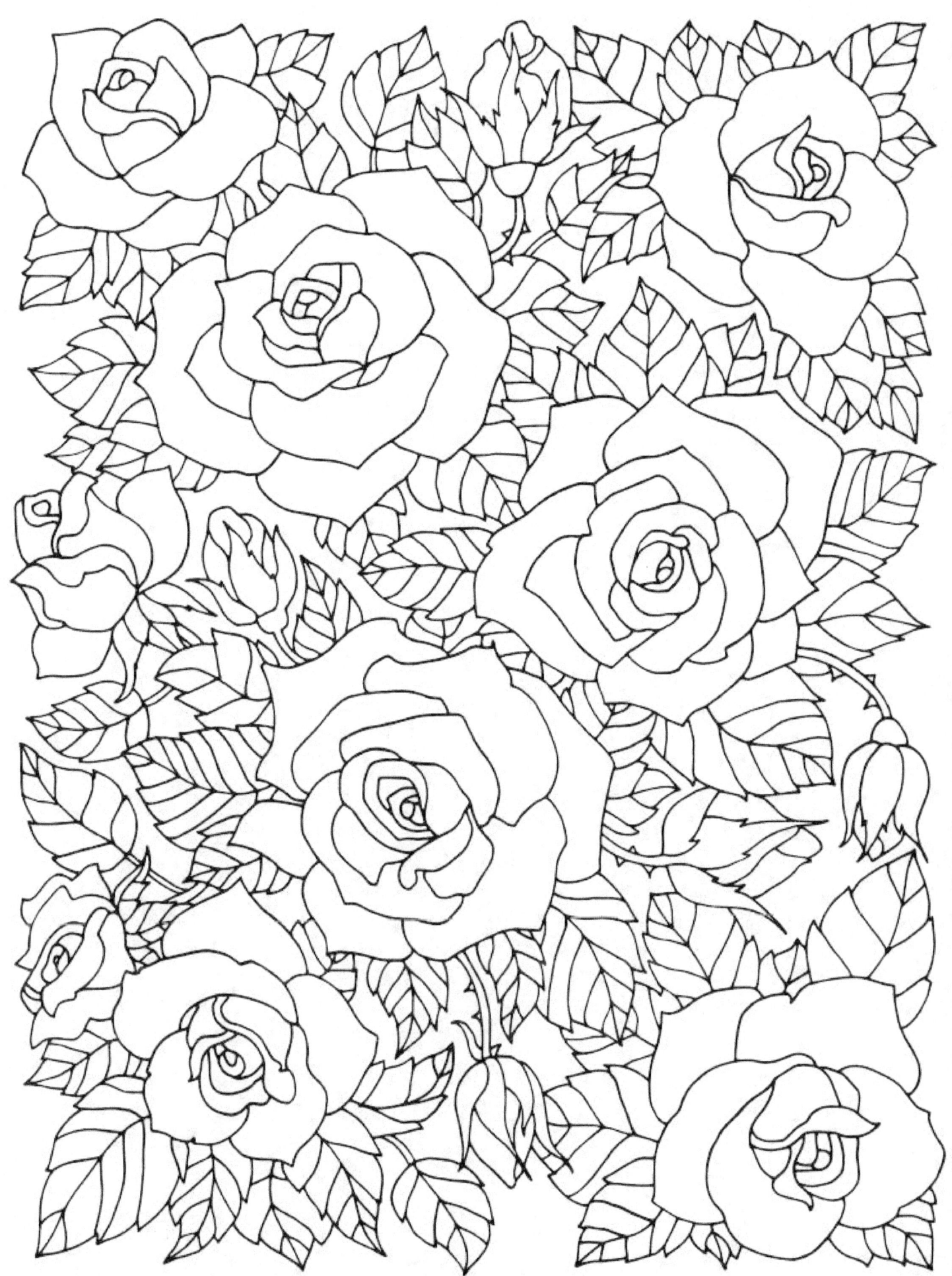

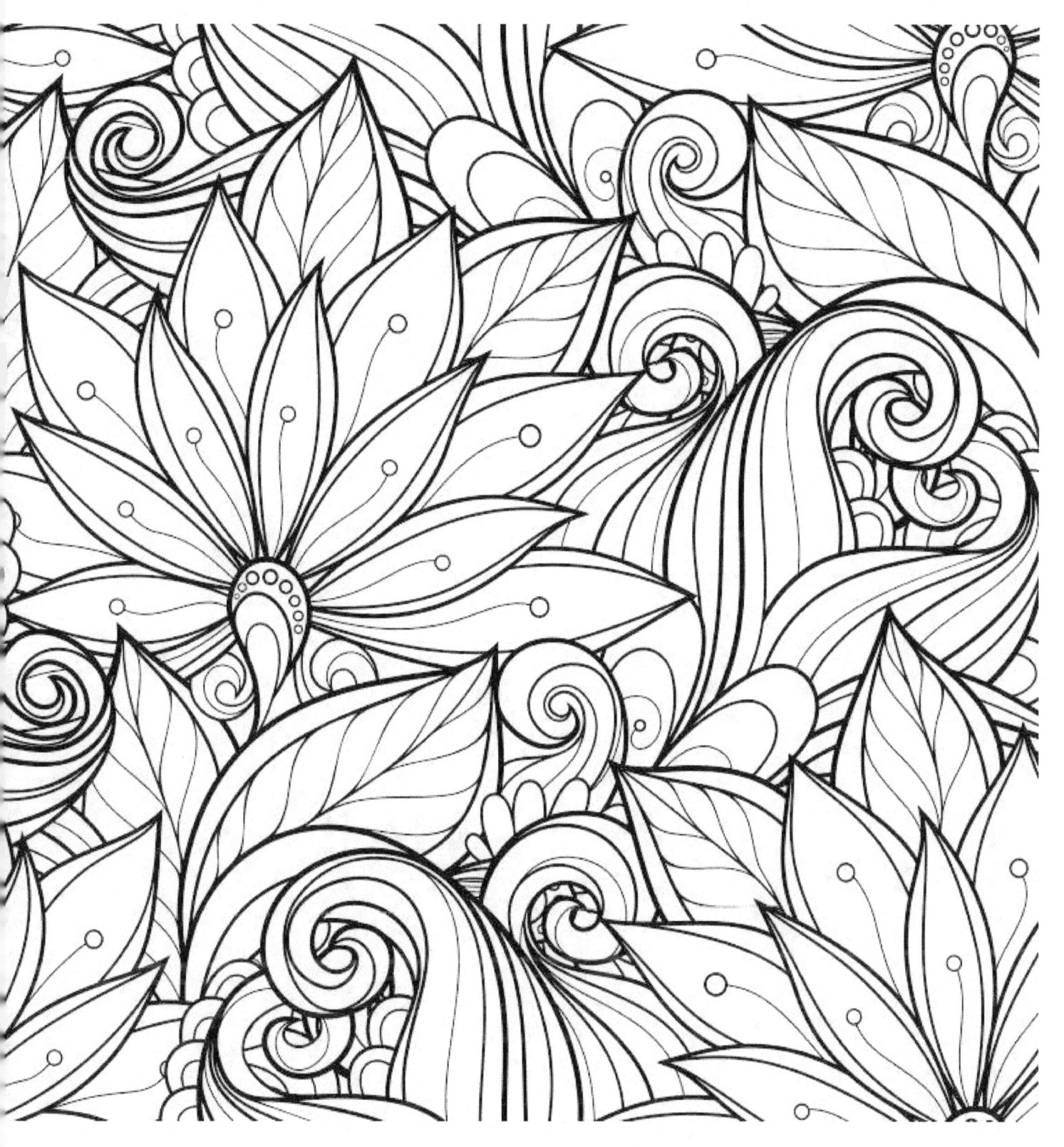

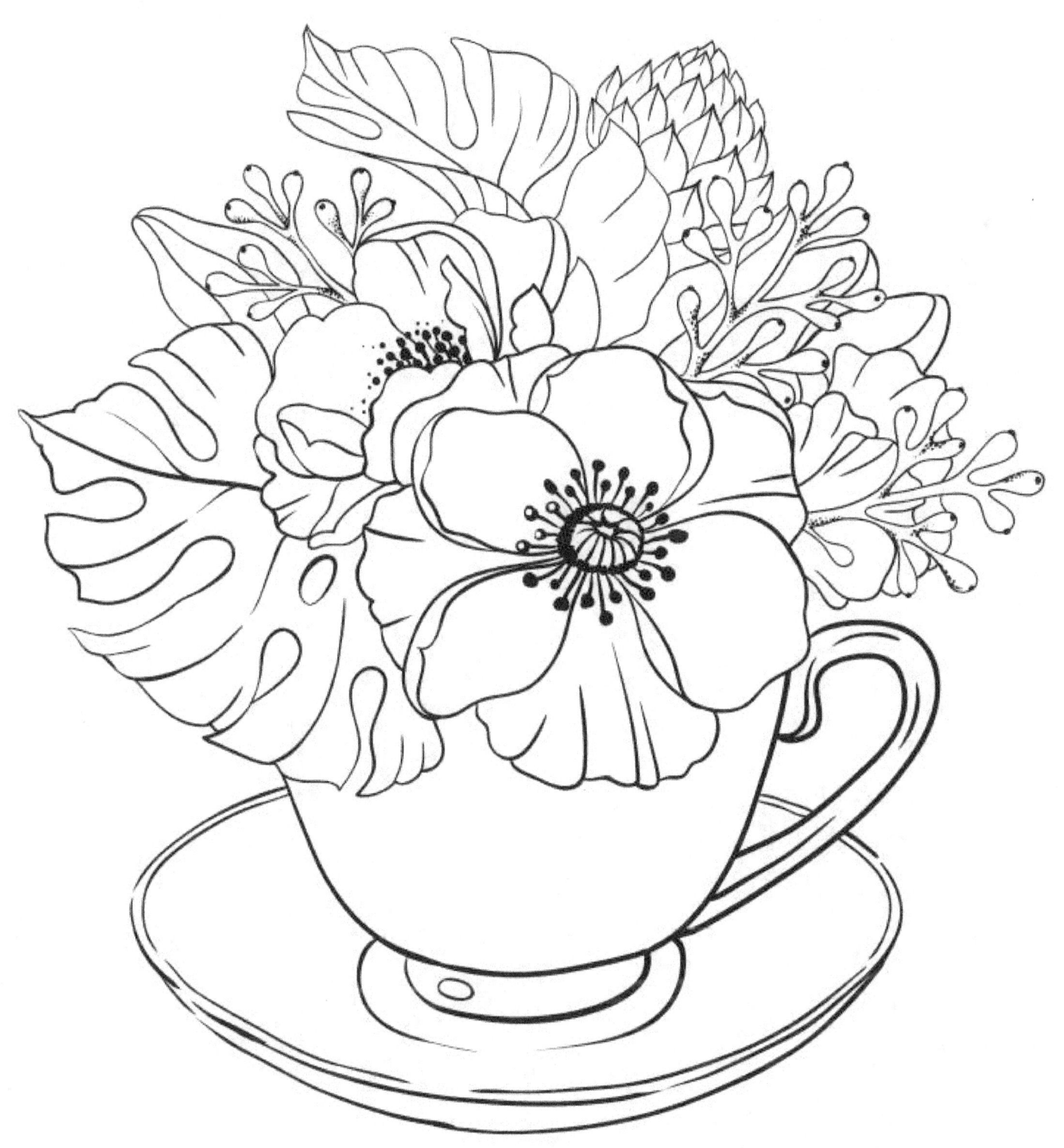

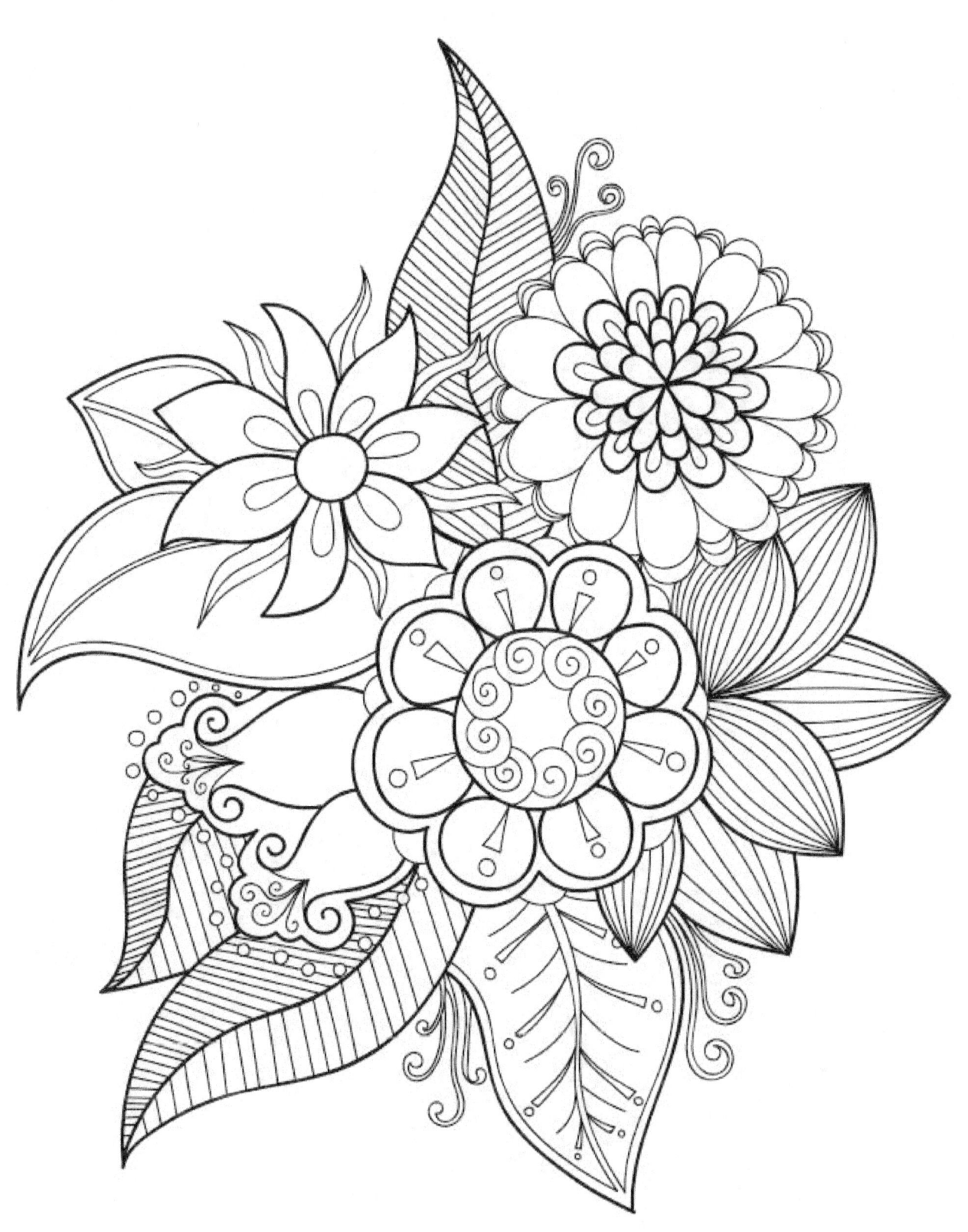

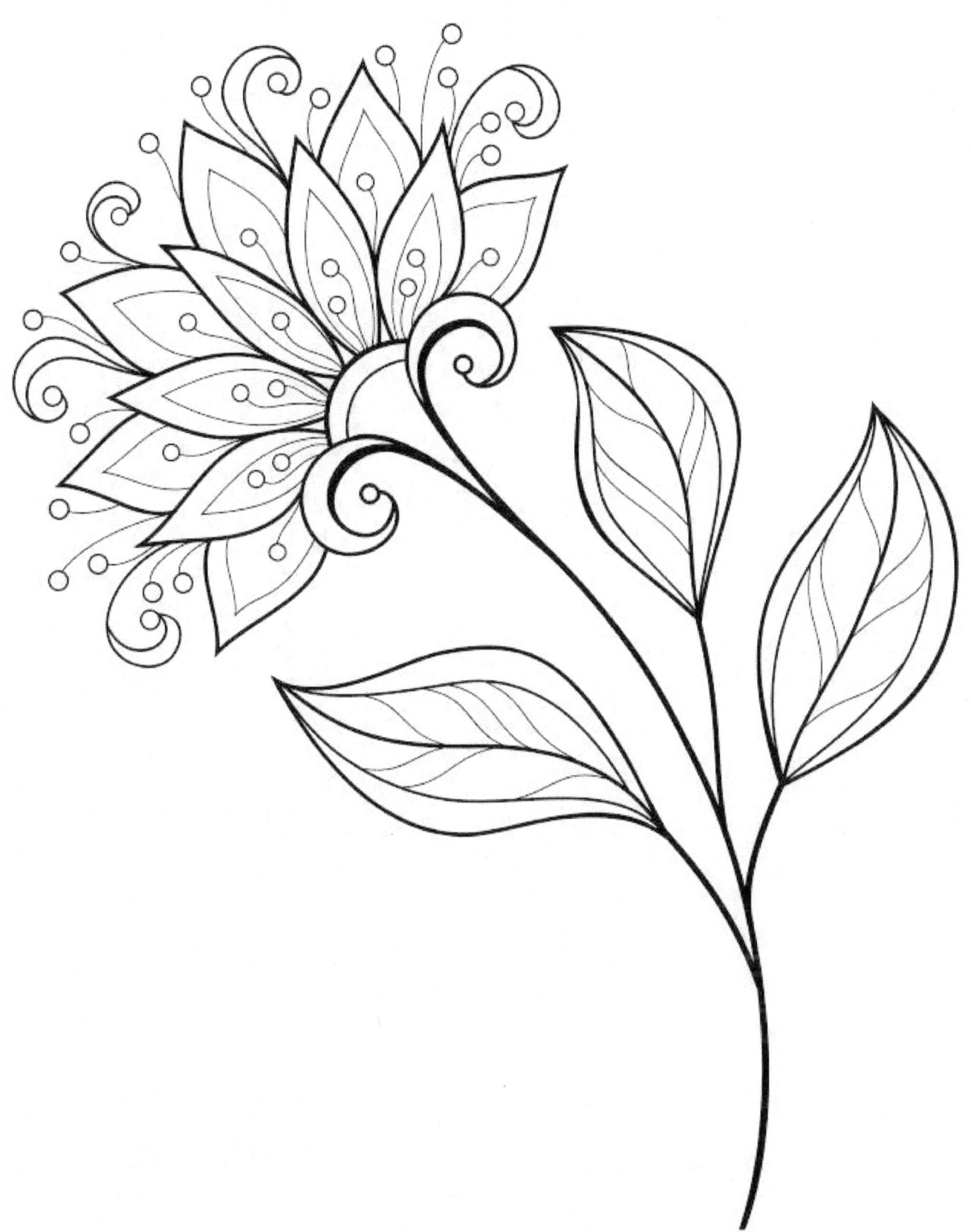

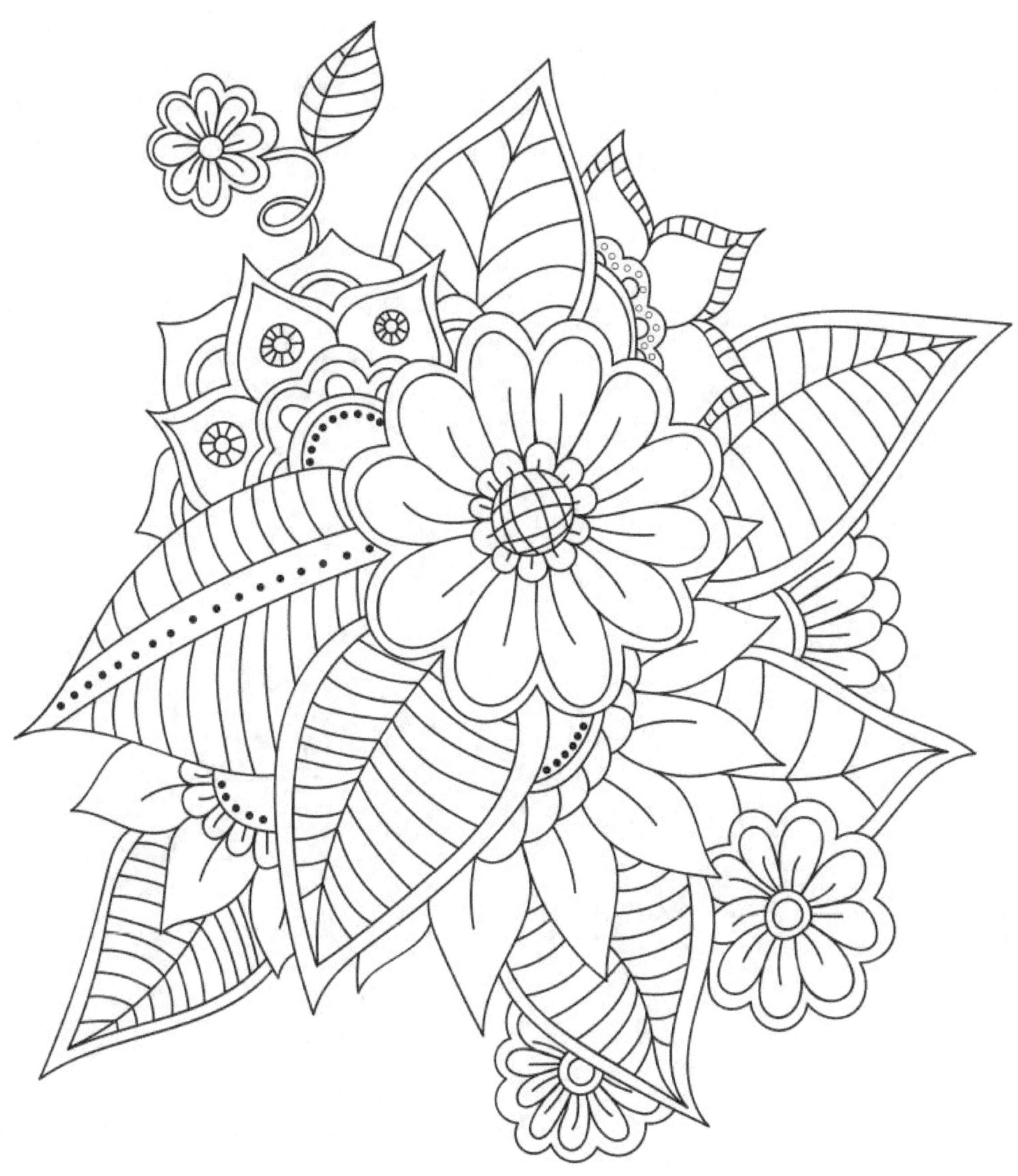

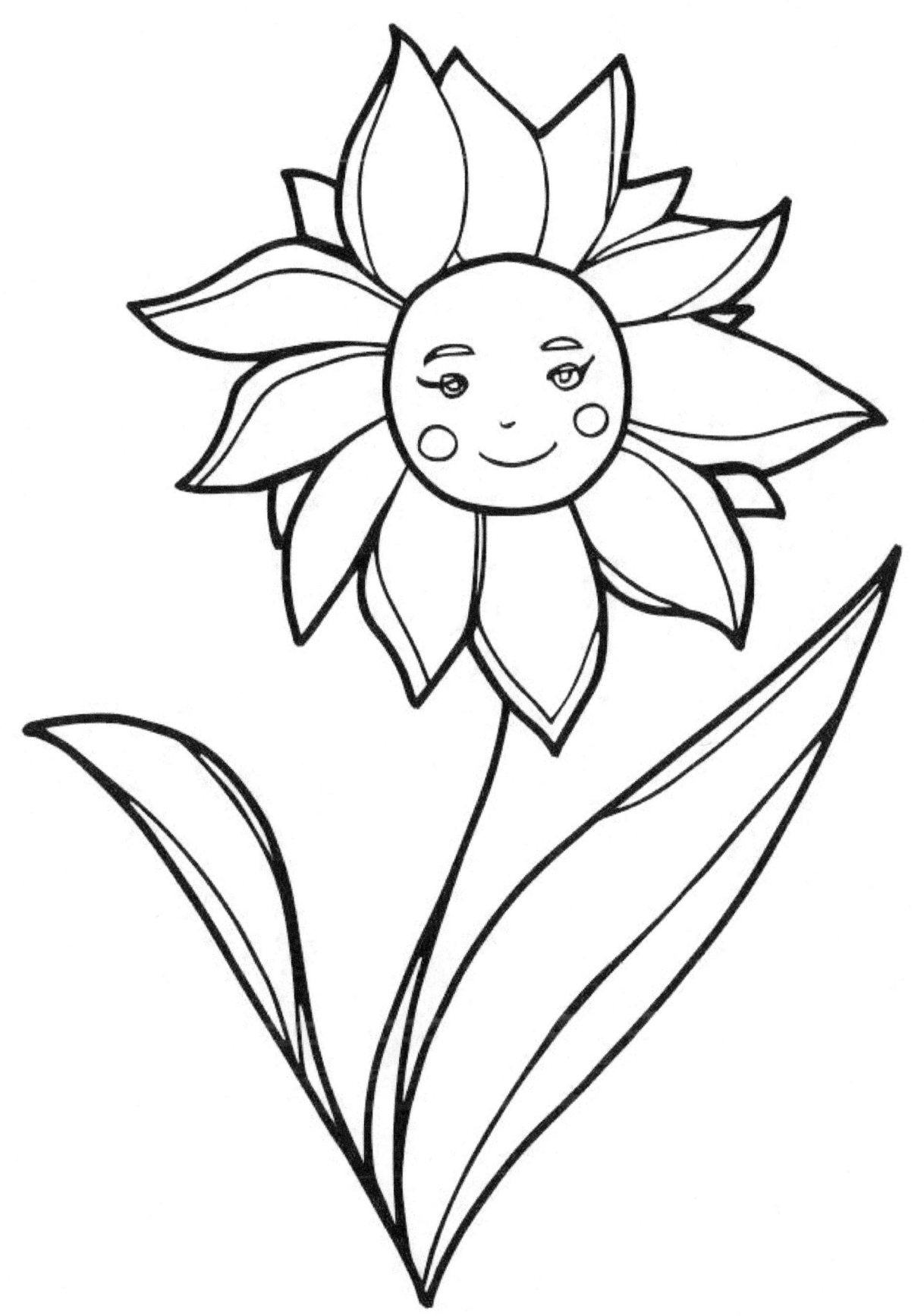

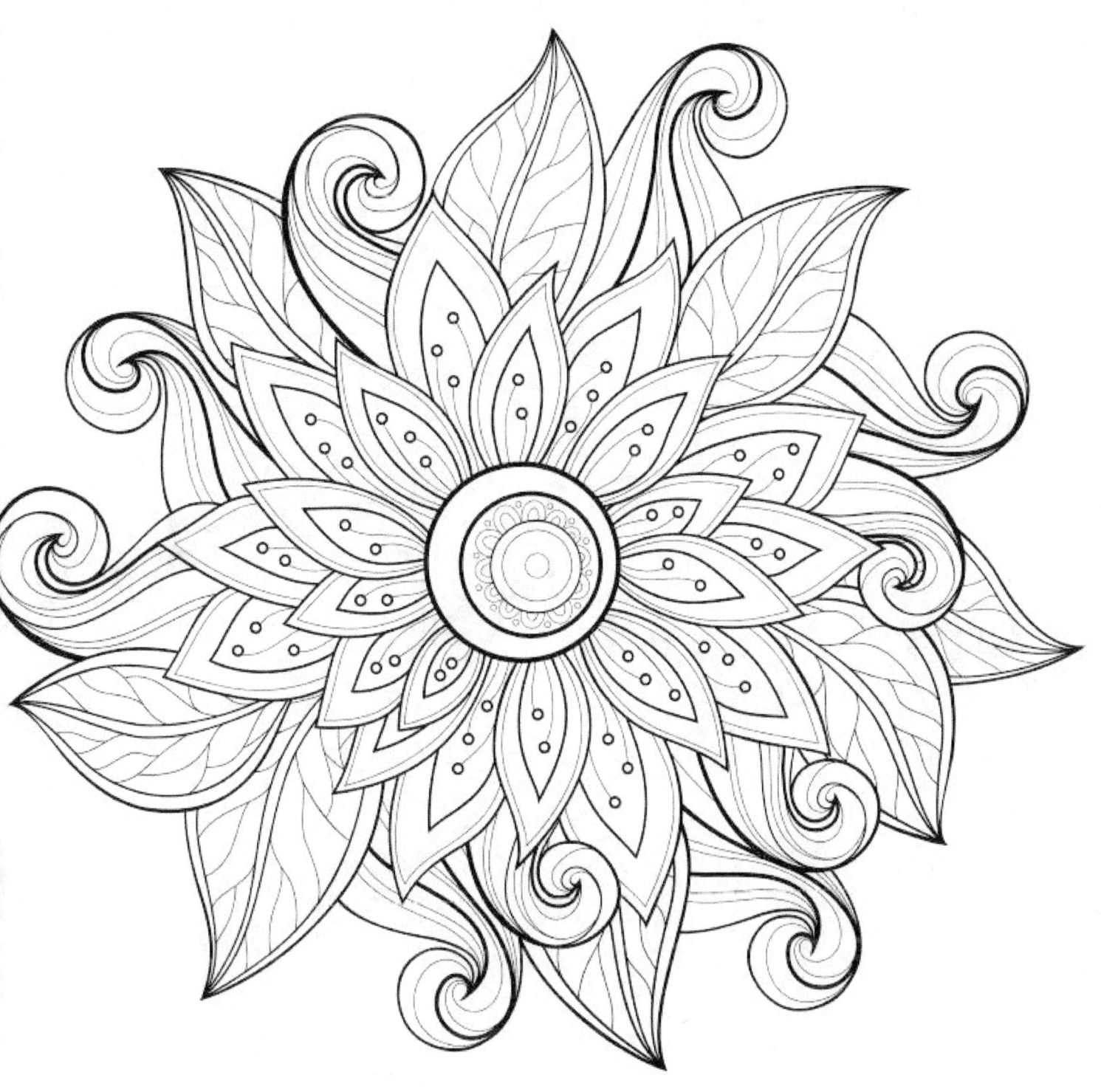

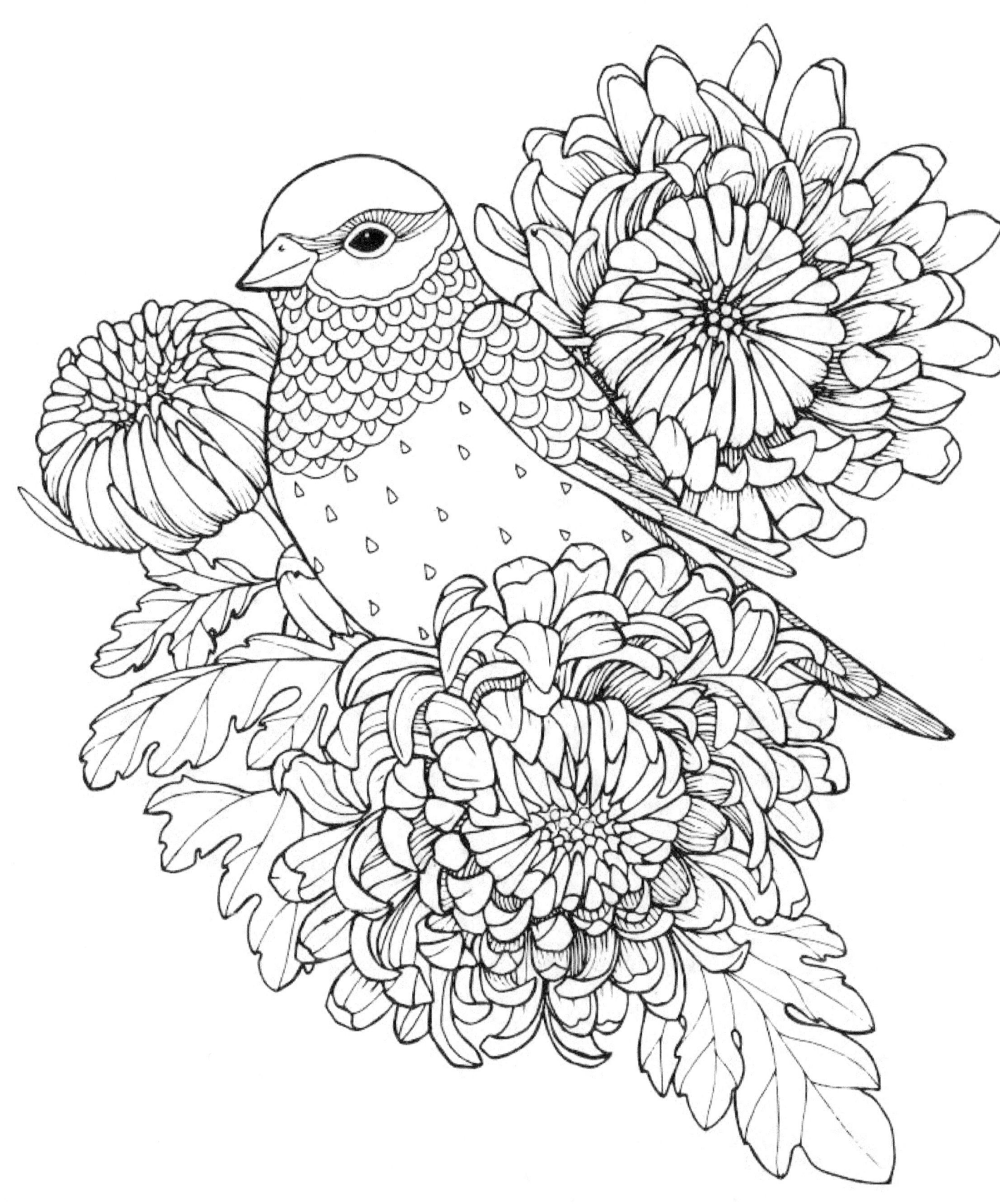

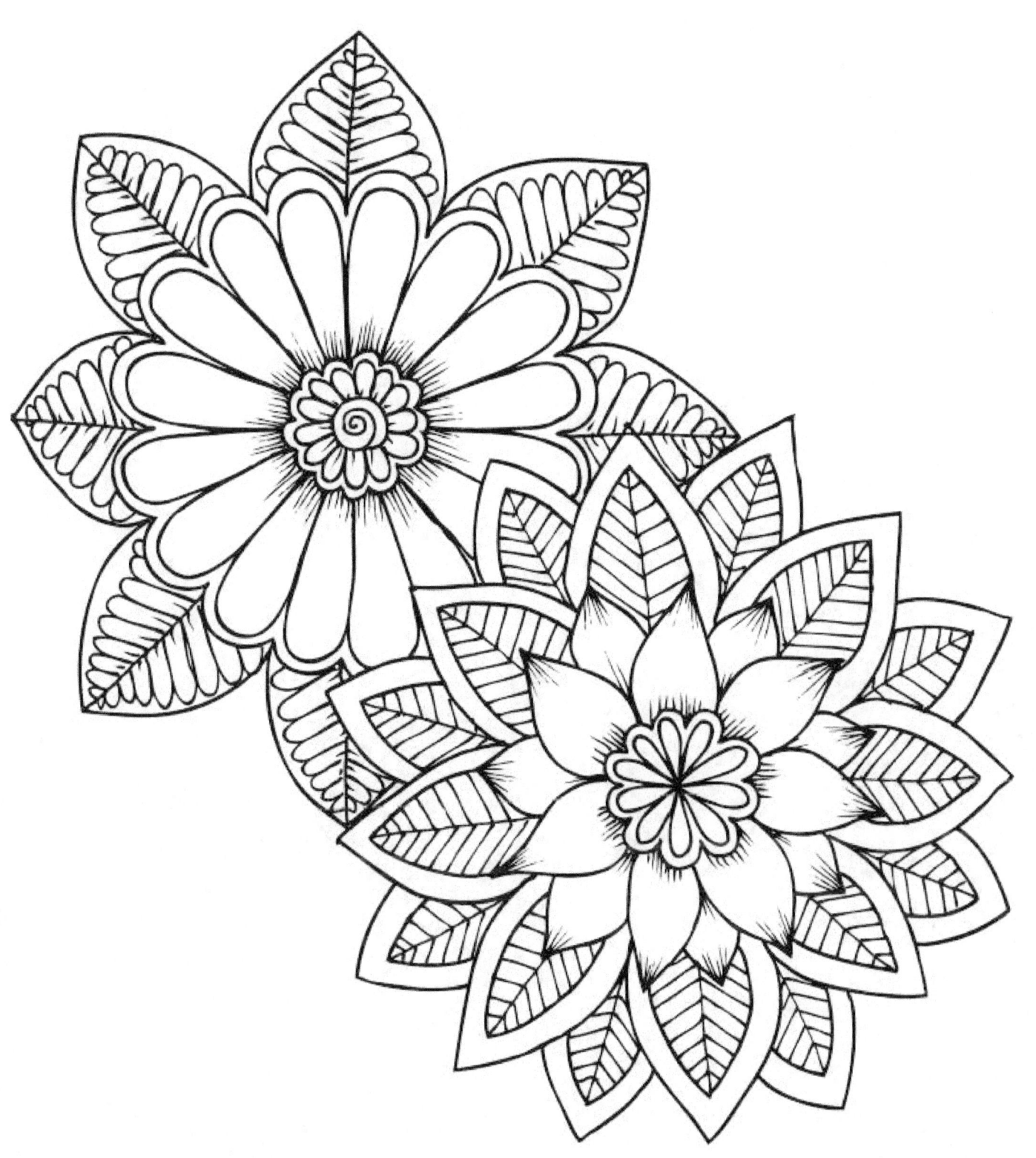

Surprise Bonus Dog Breeds and Beautiful Sea Turtles Coloring Pages!

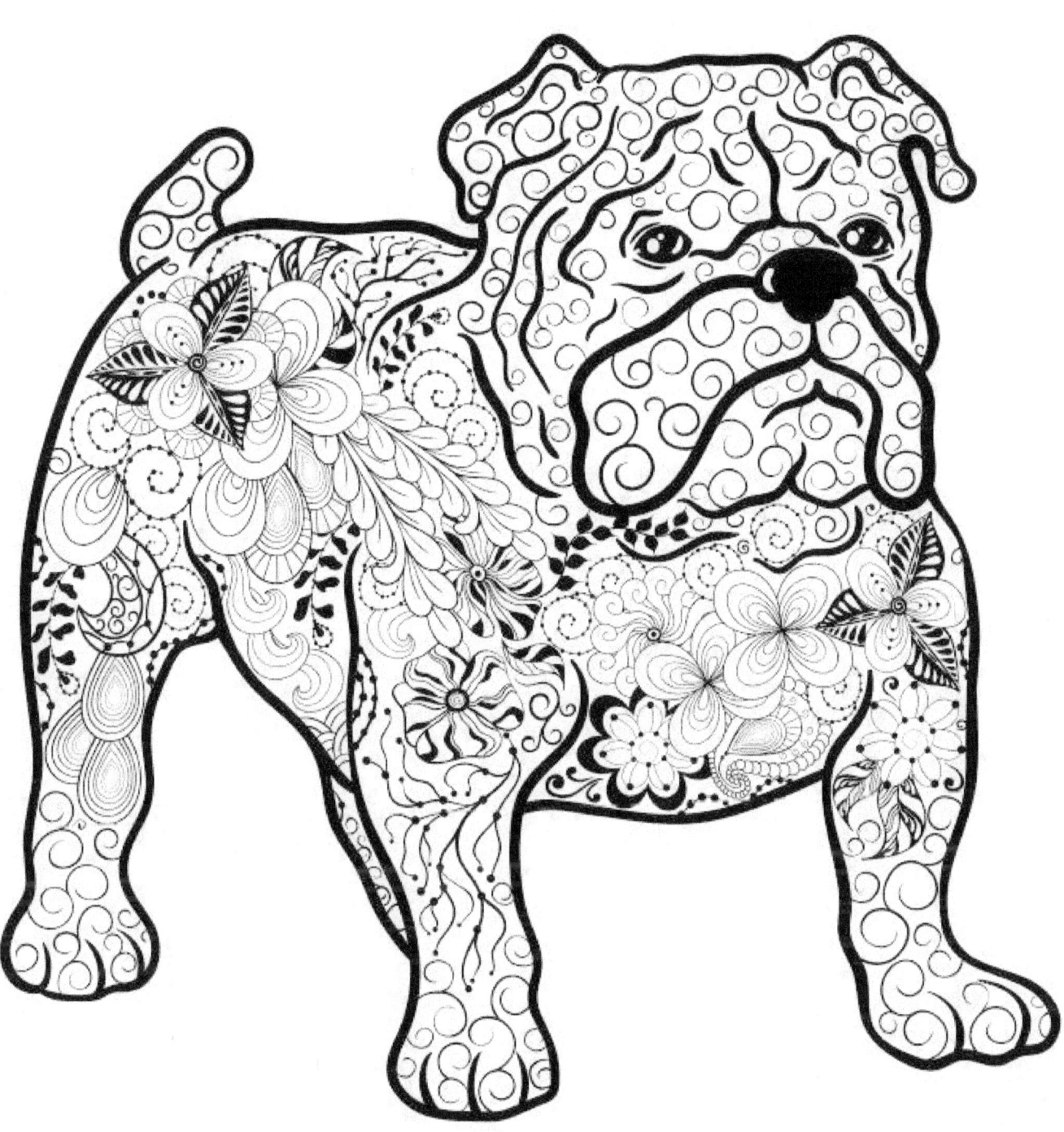

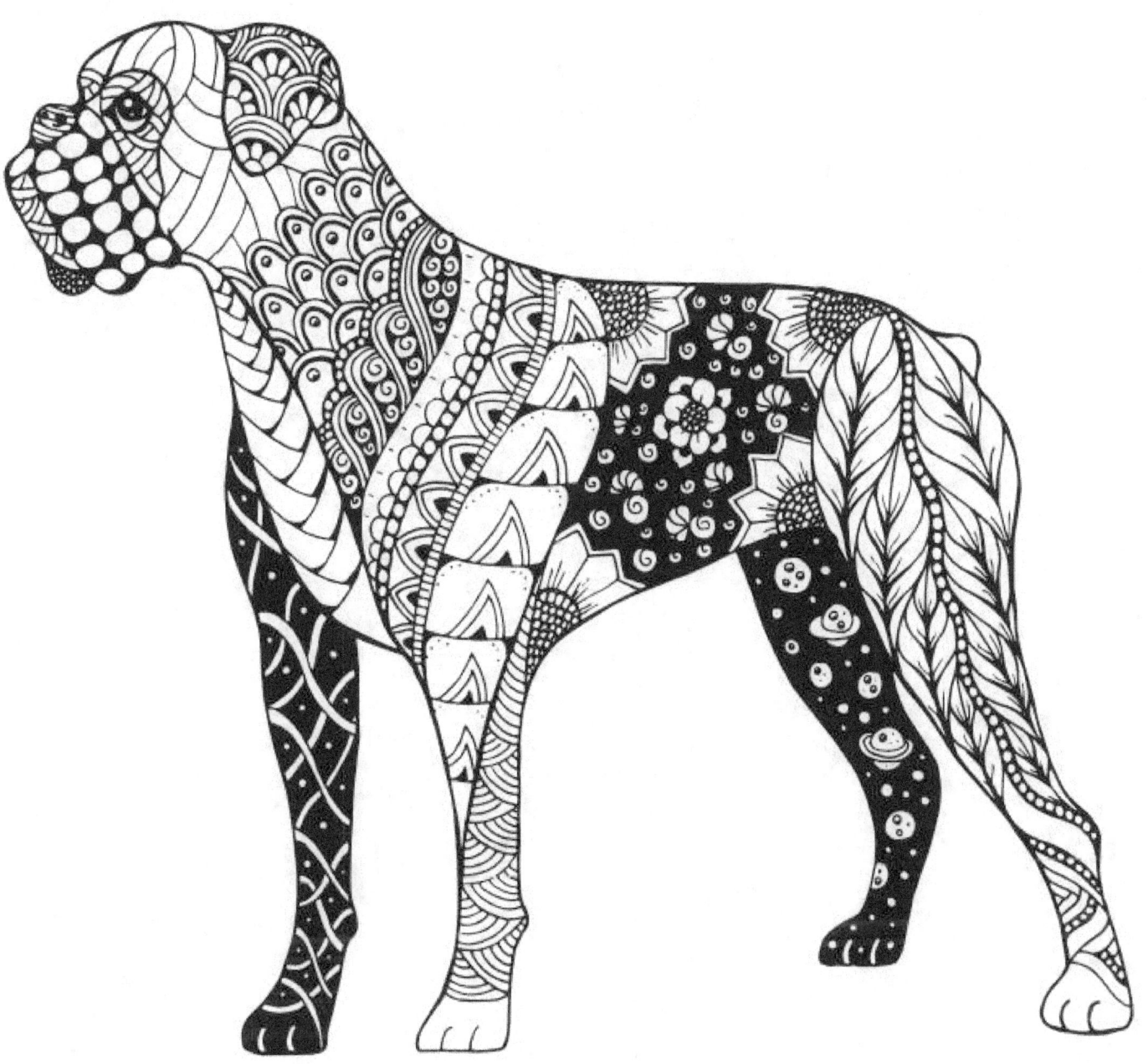

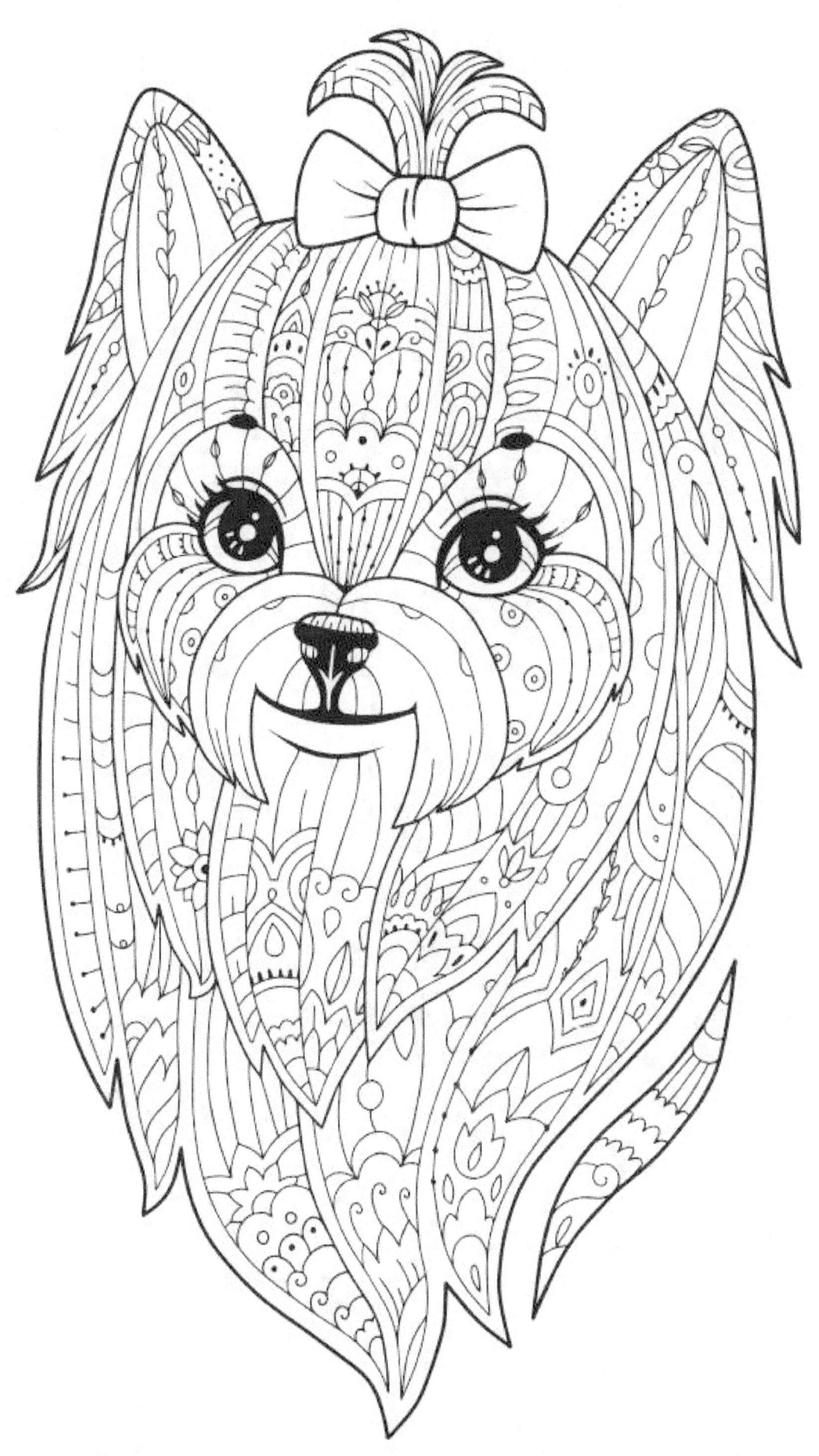

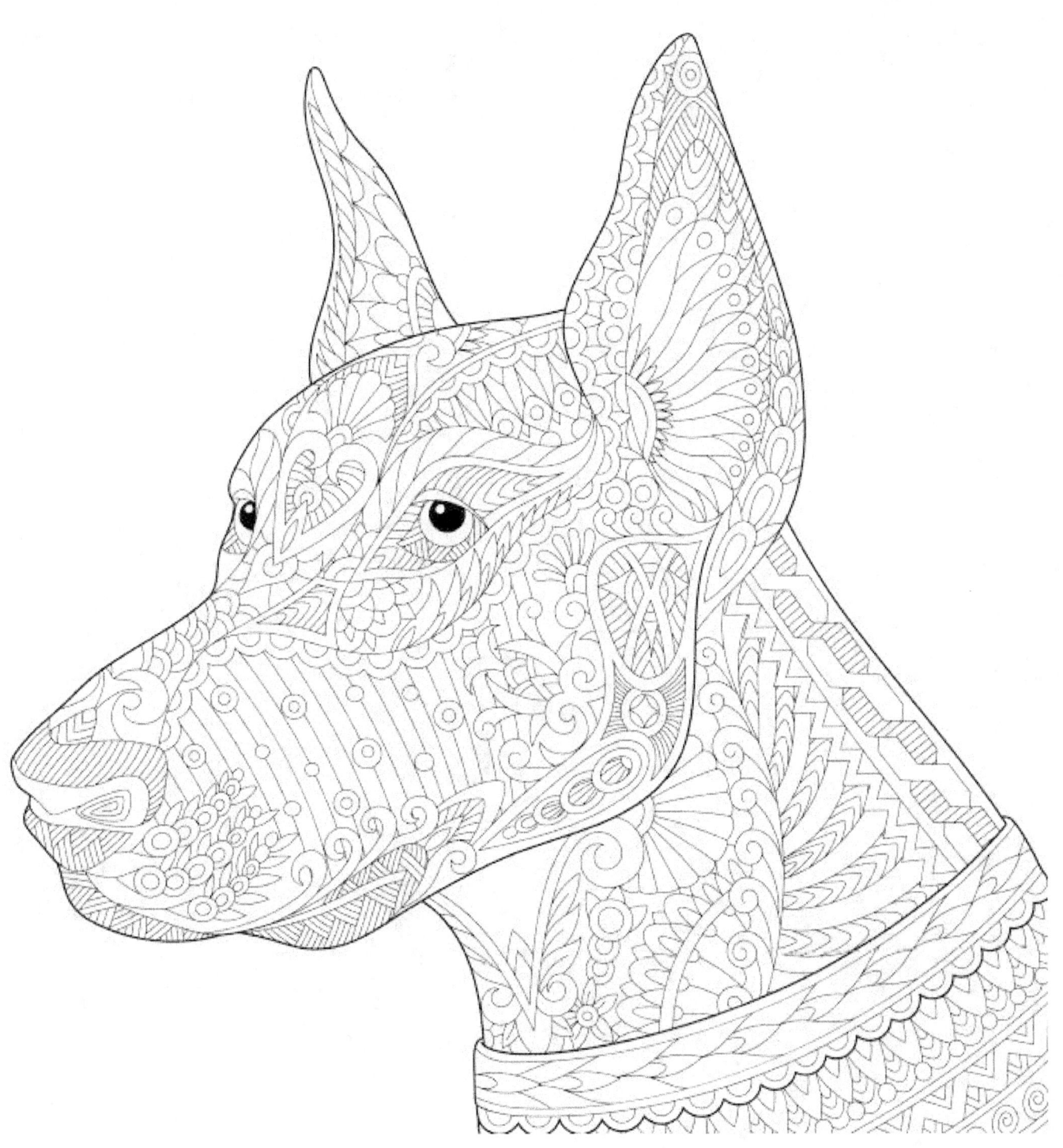

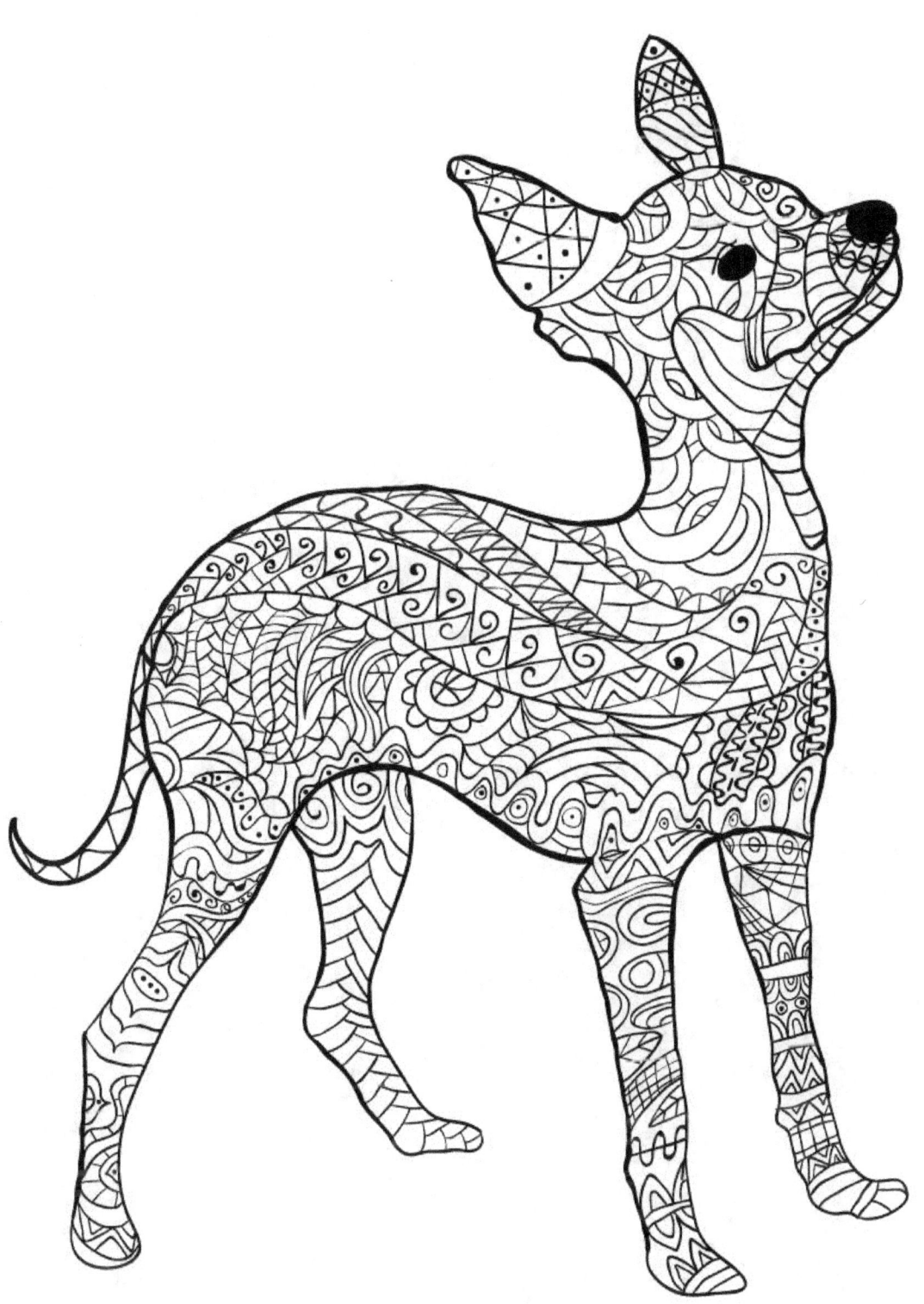

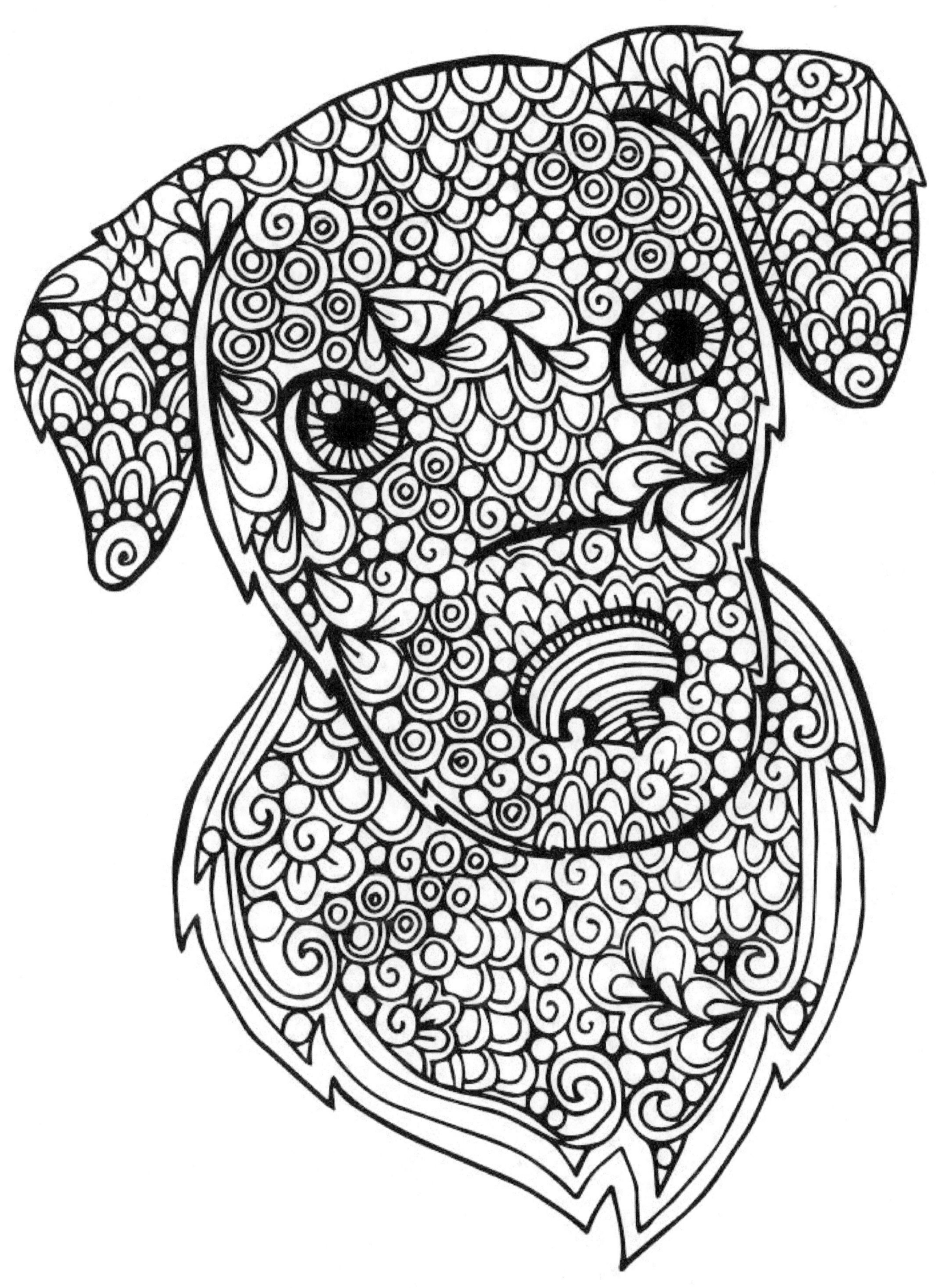

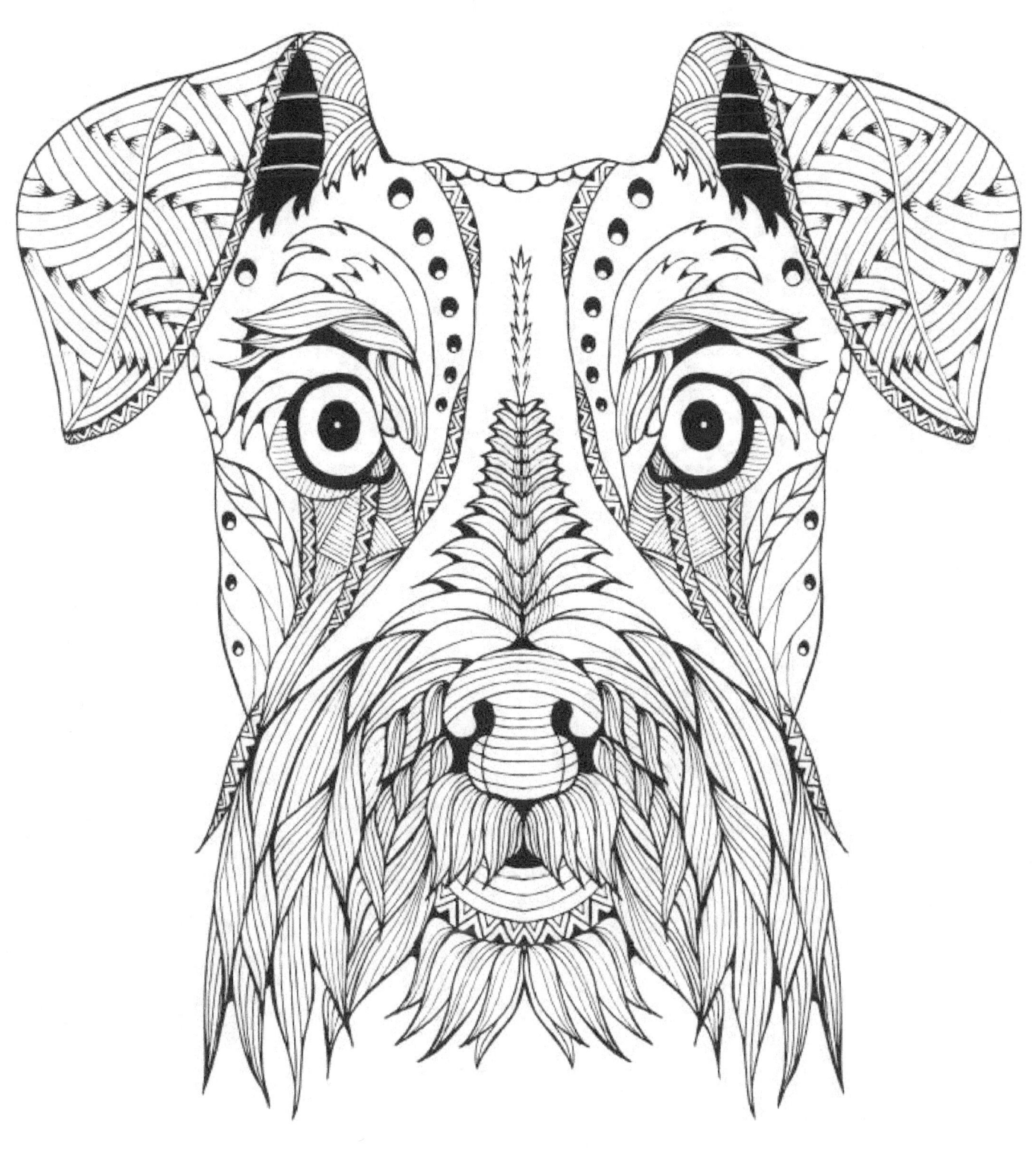

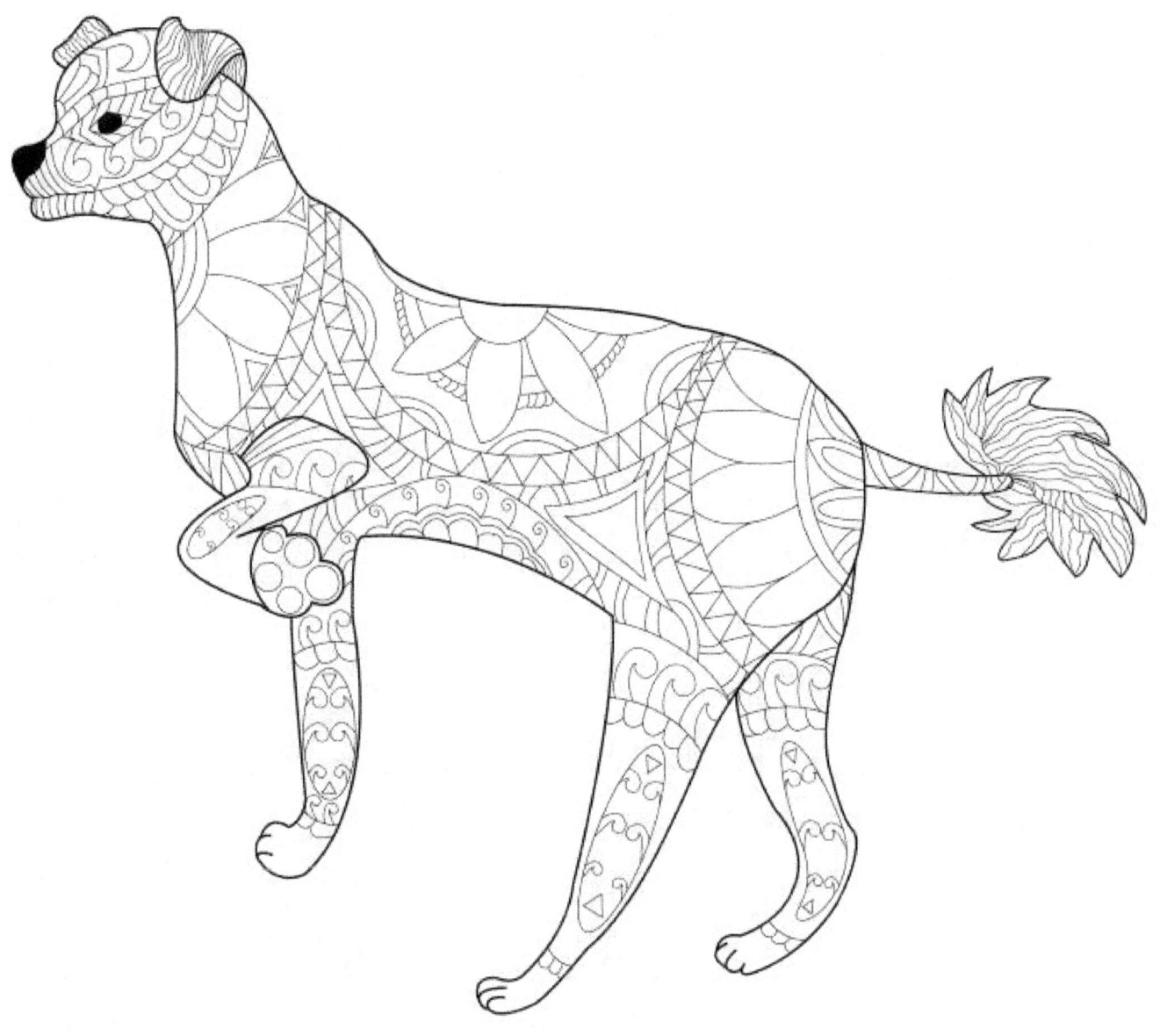

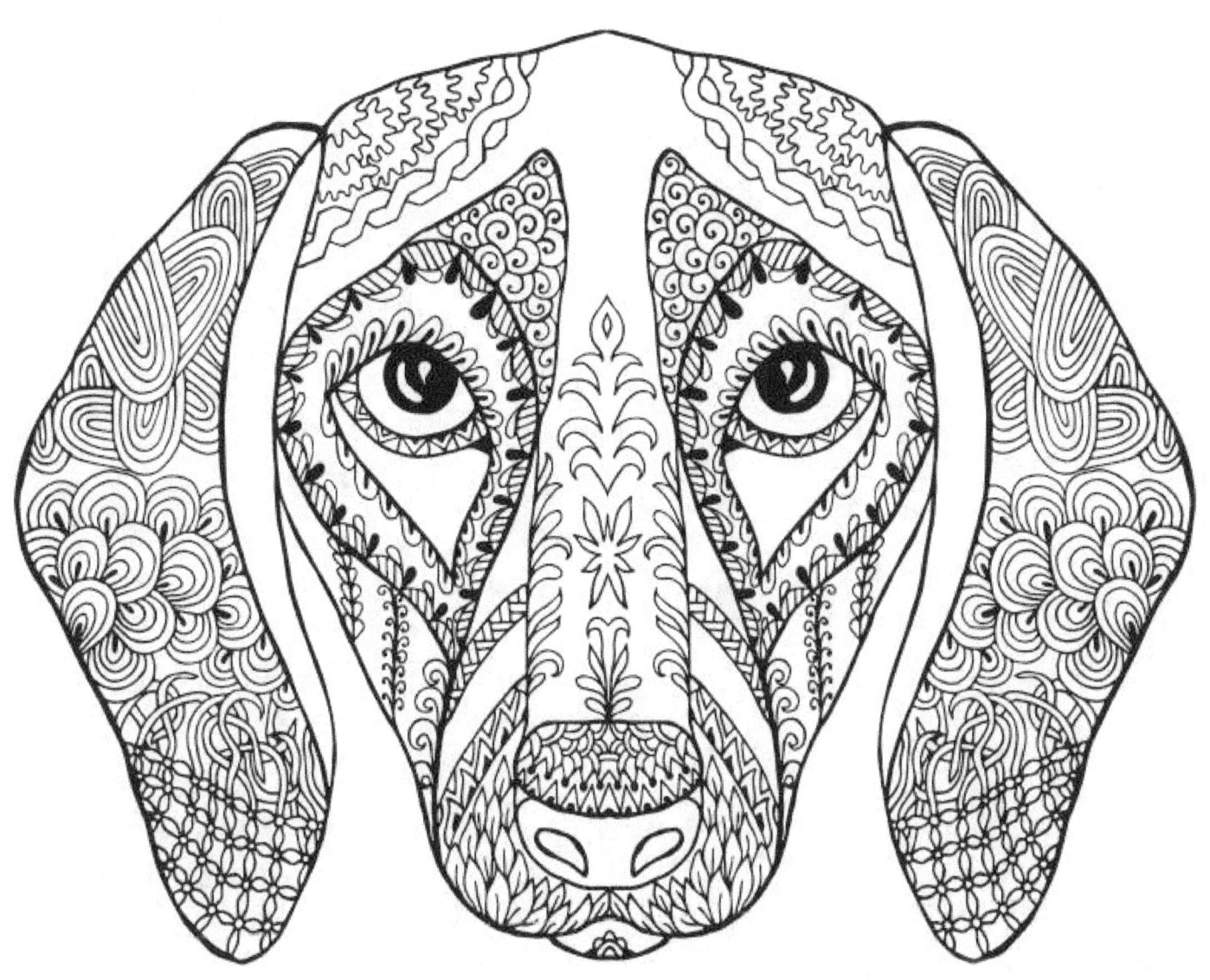

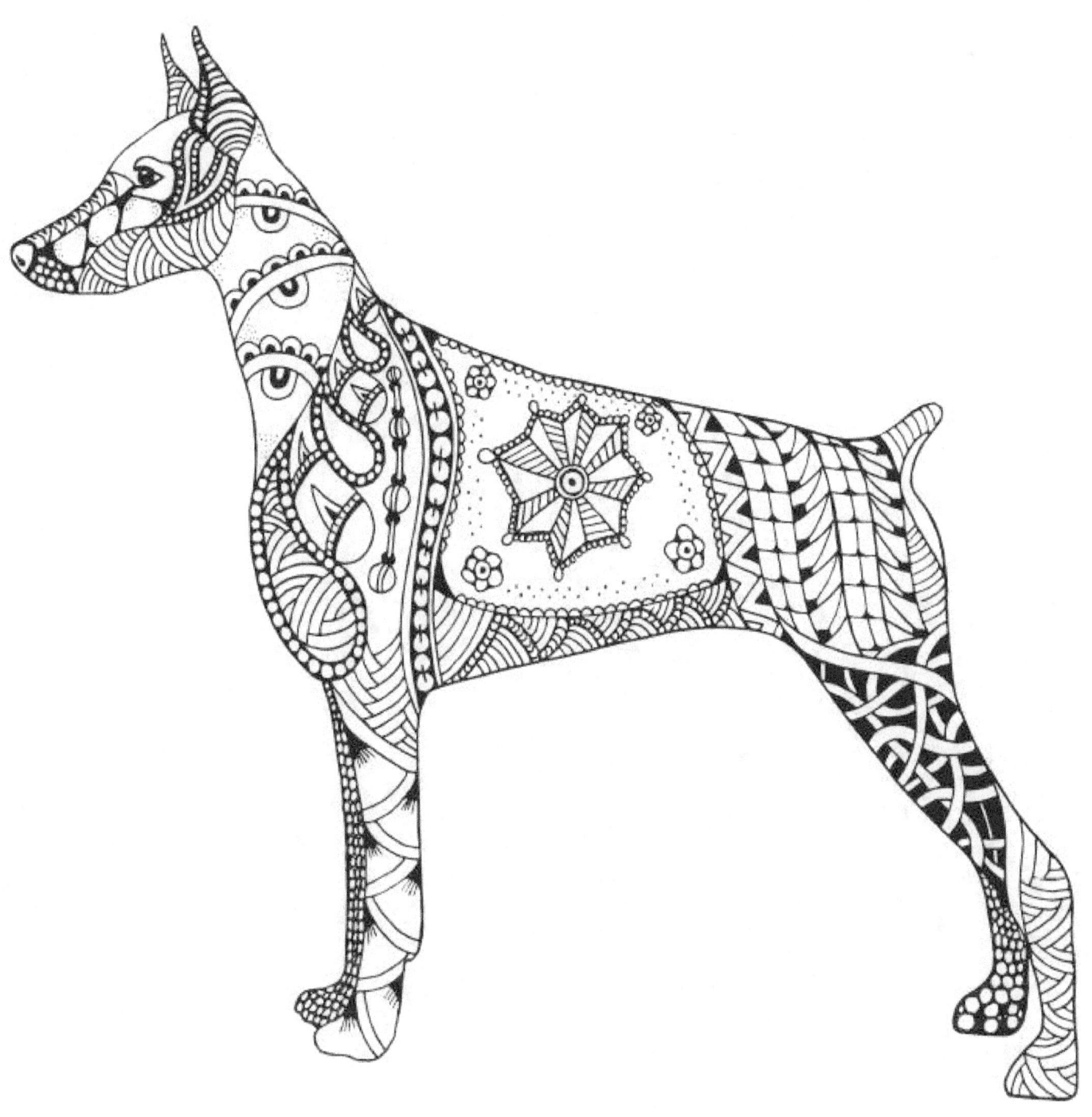

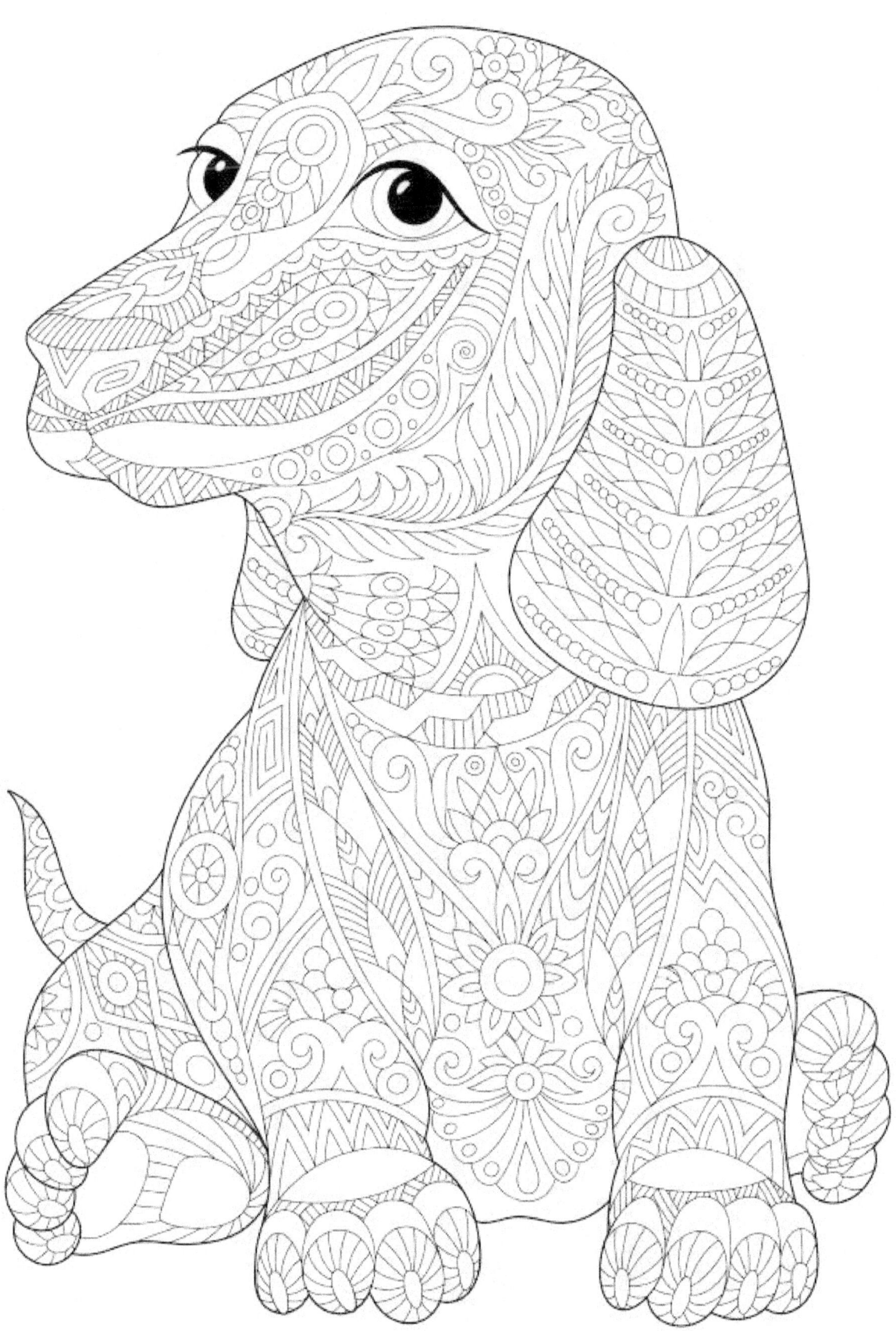

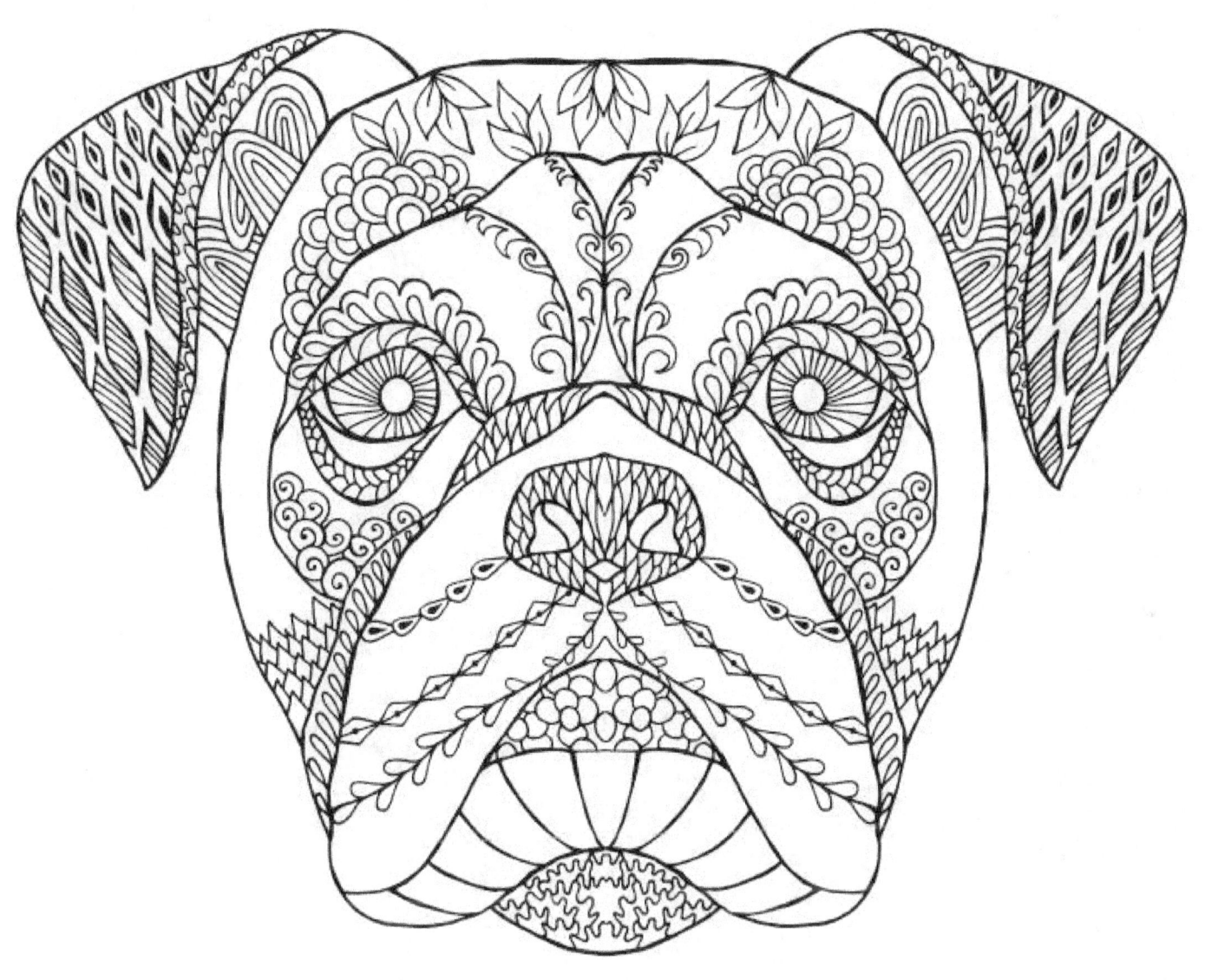

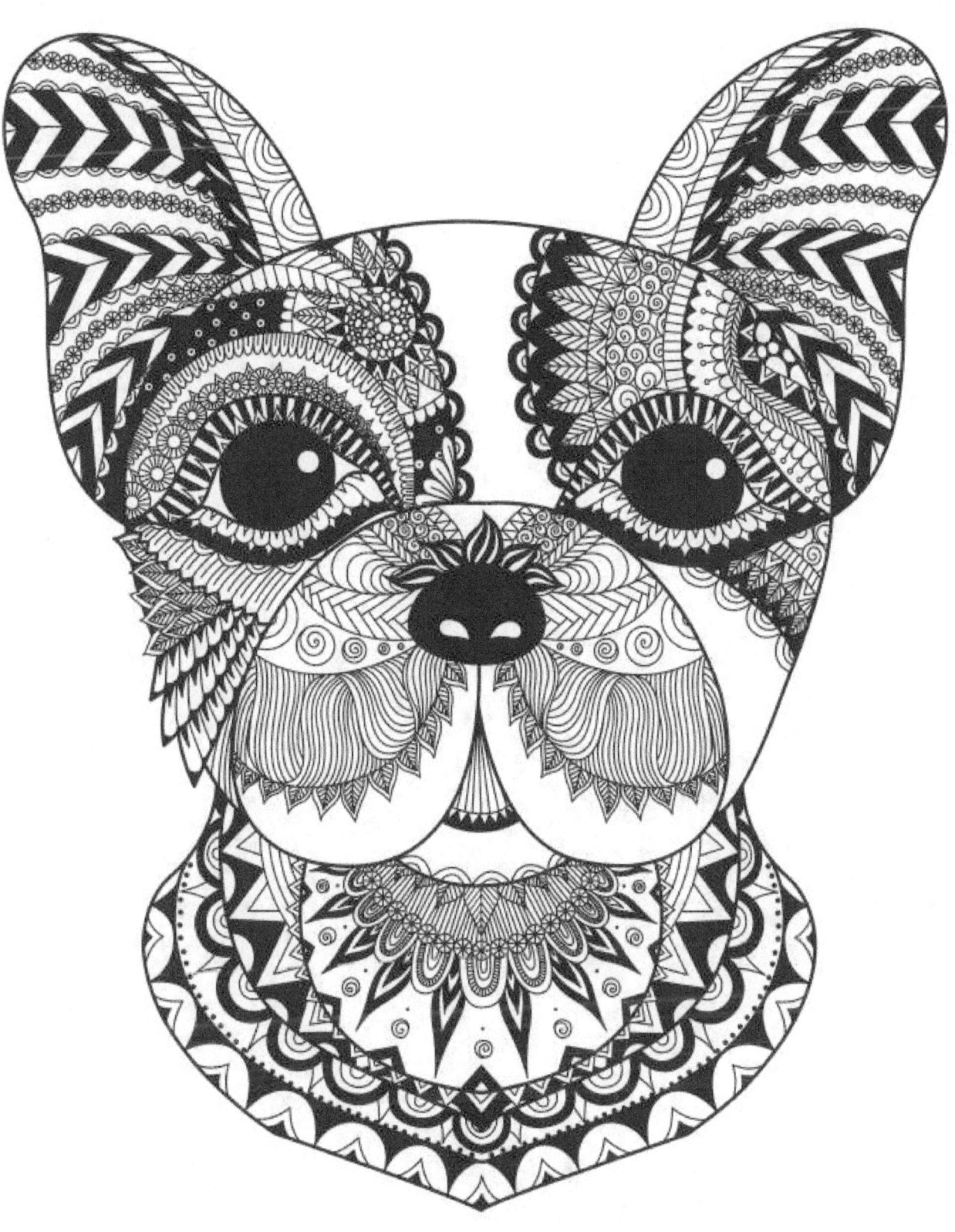

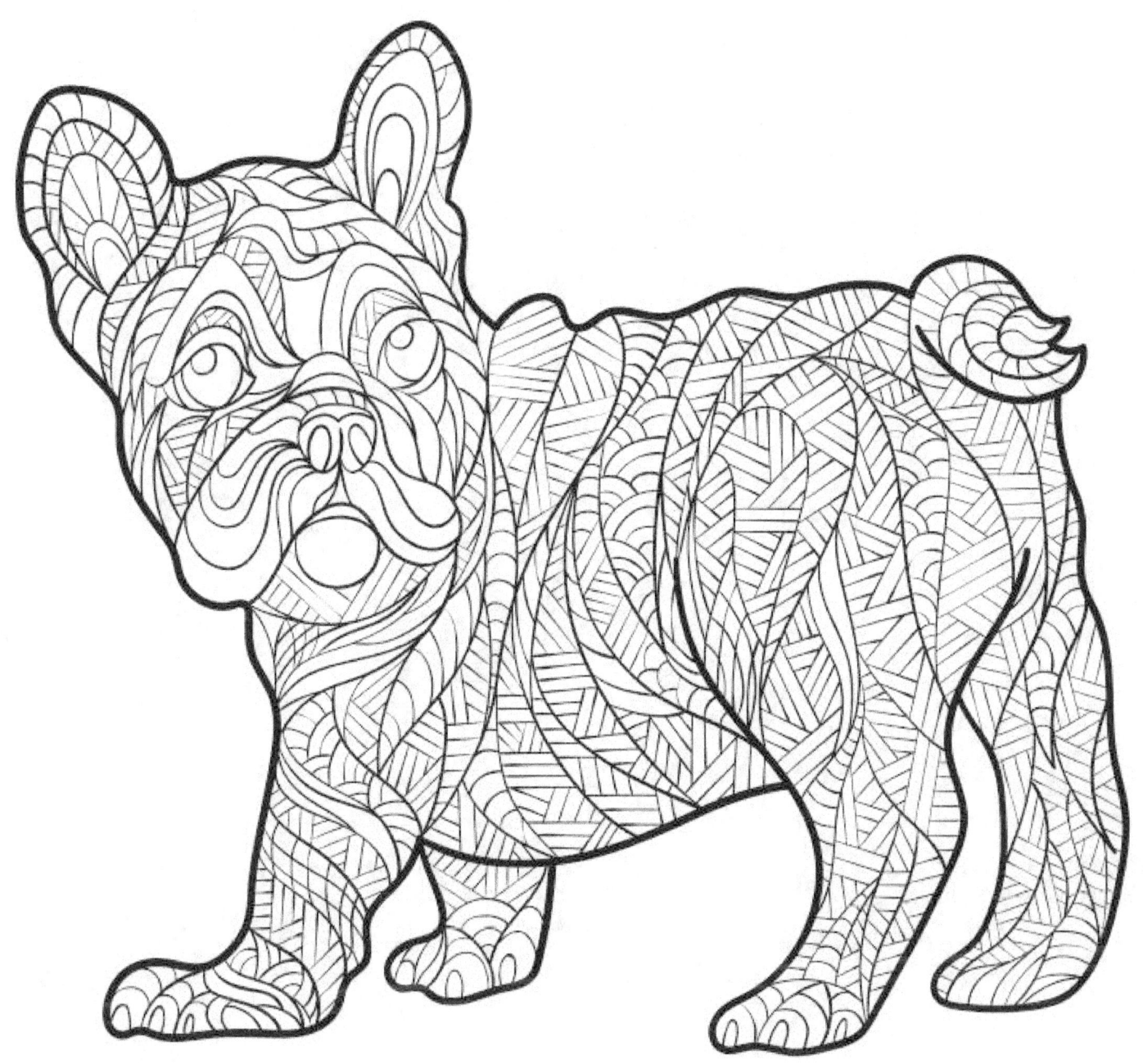

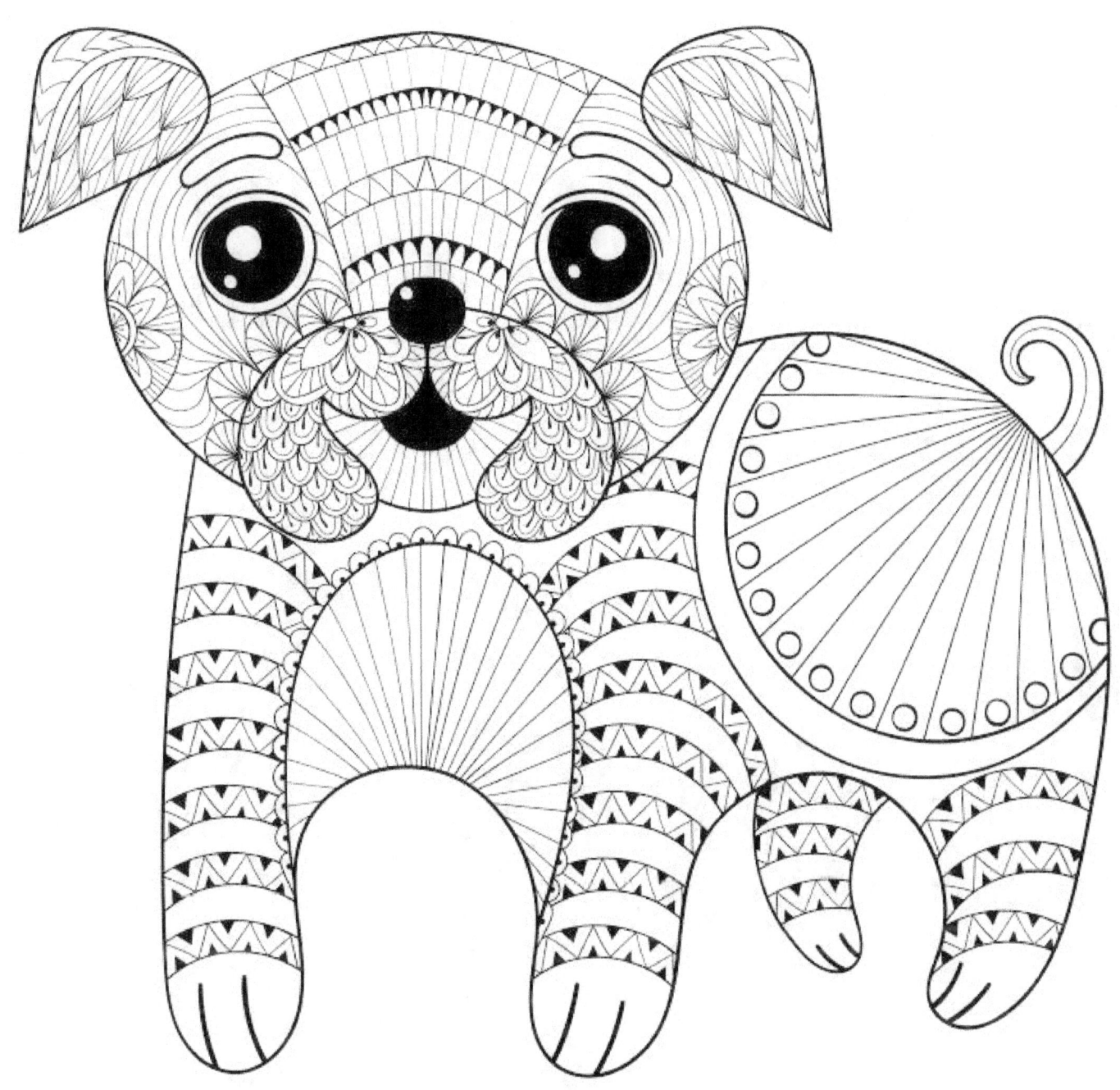

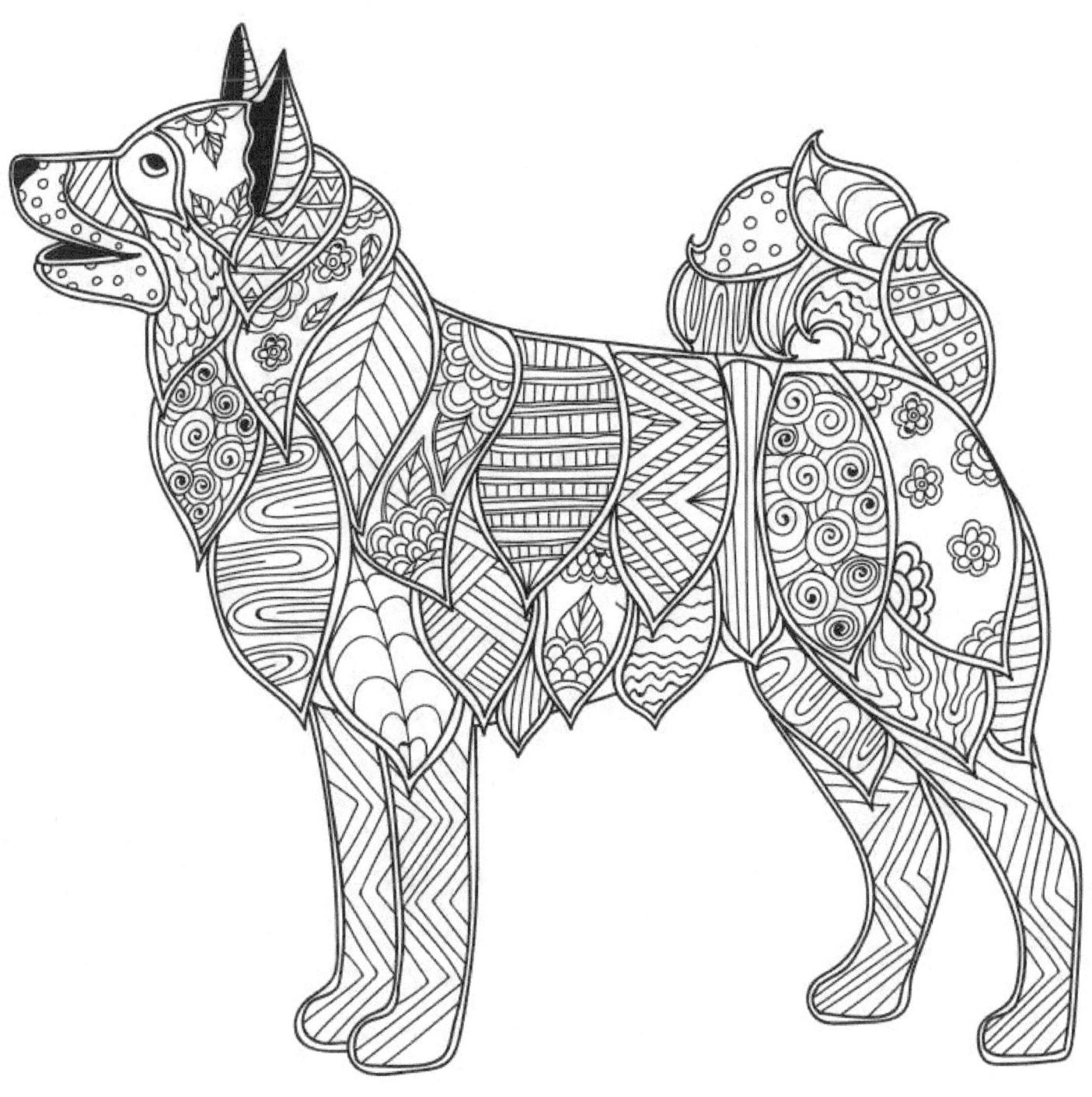

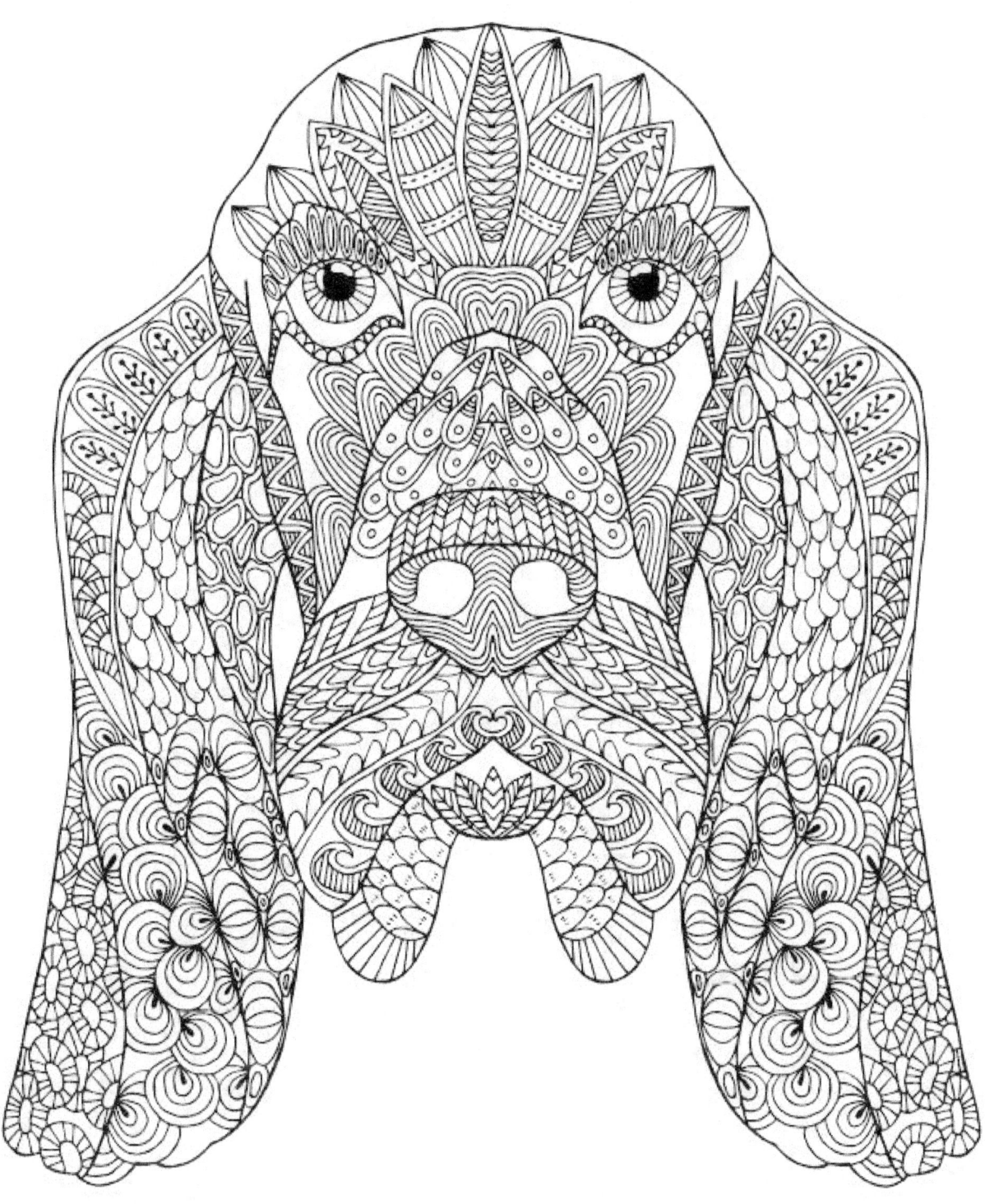

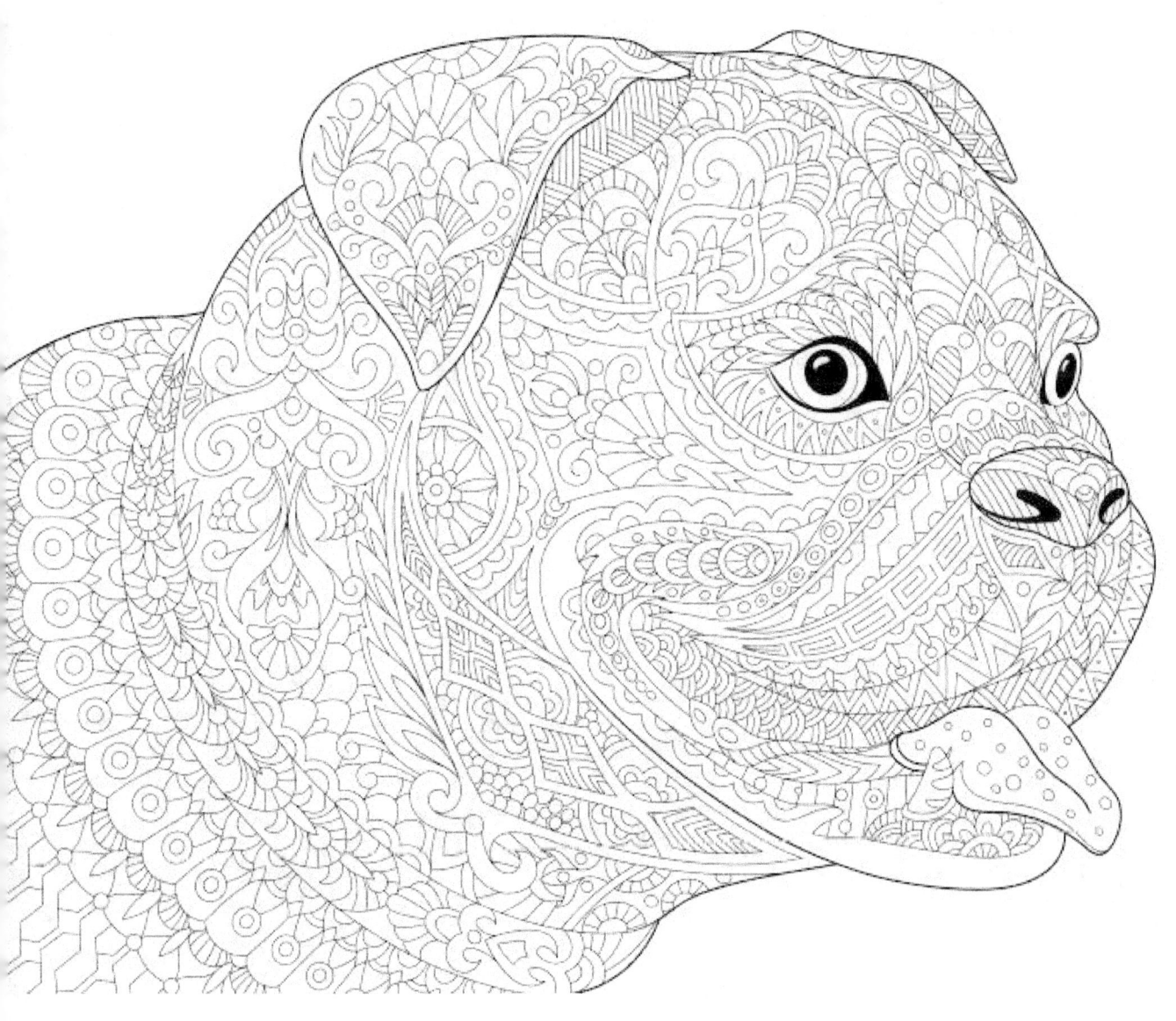

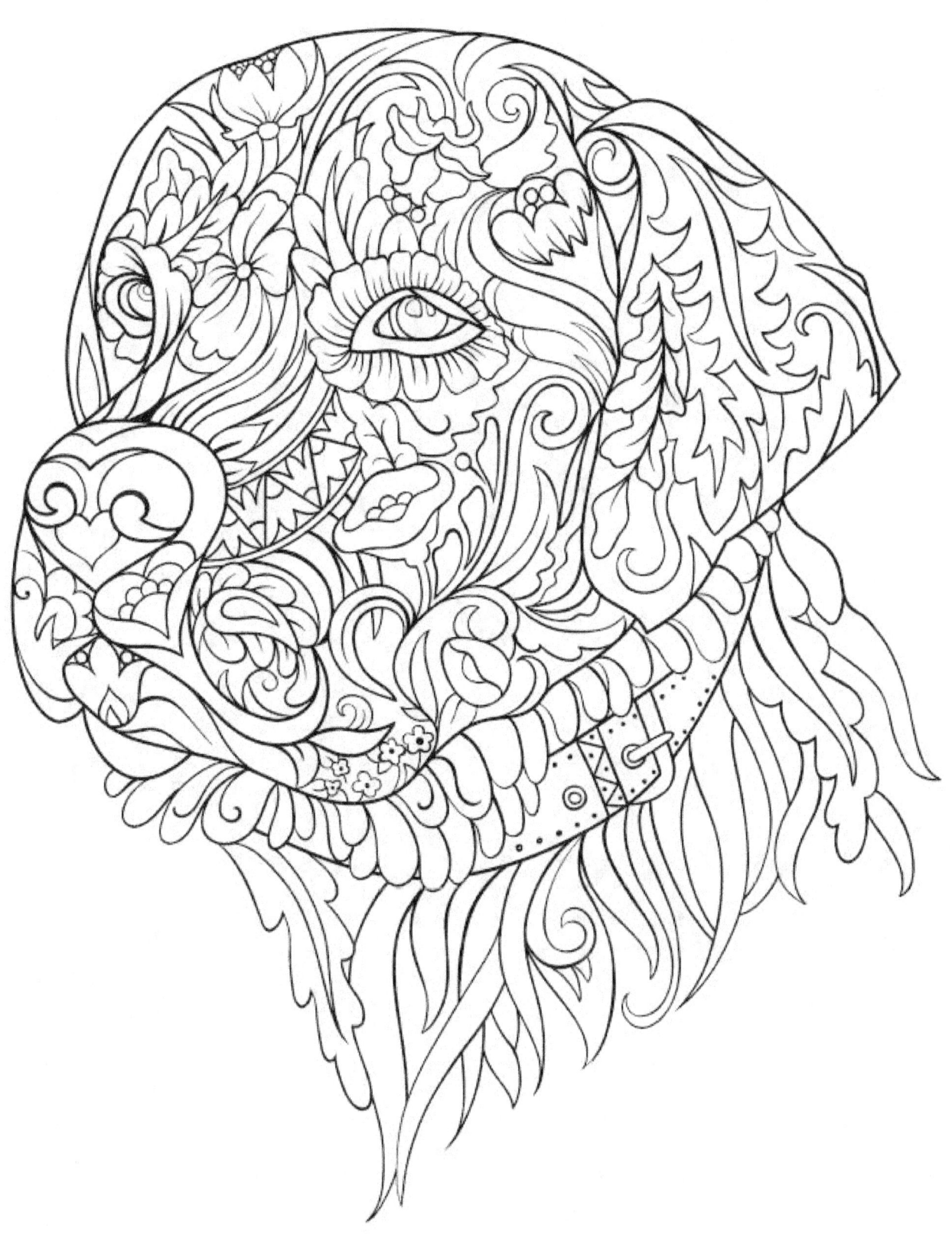

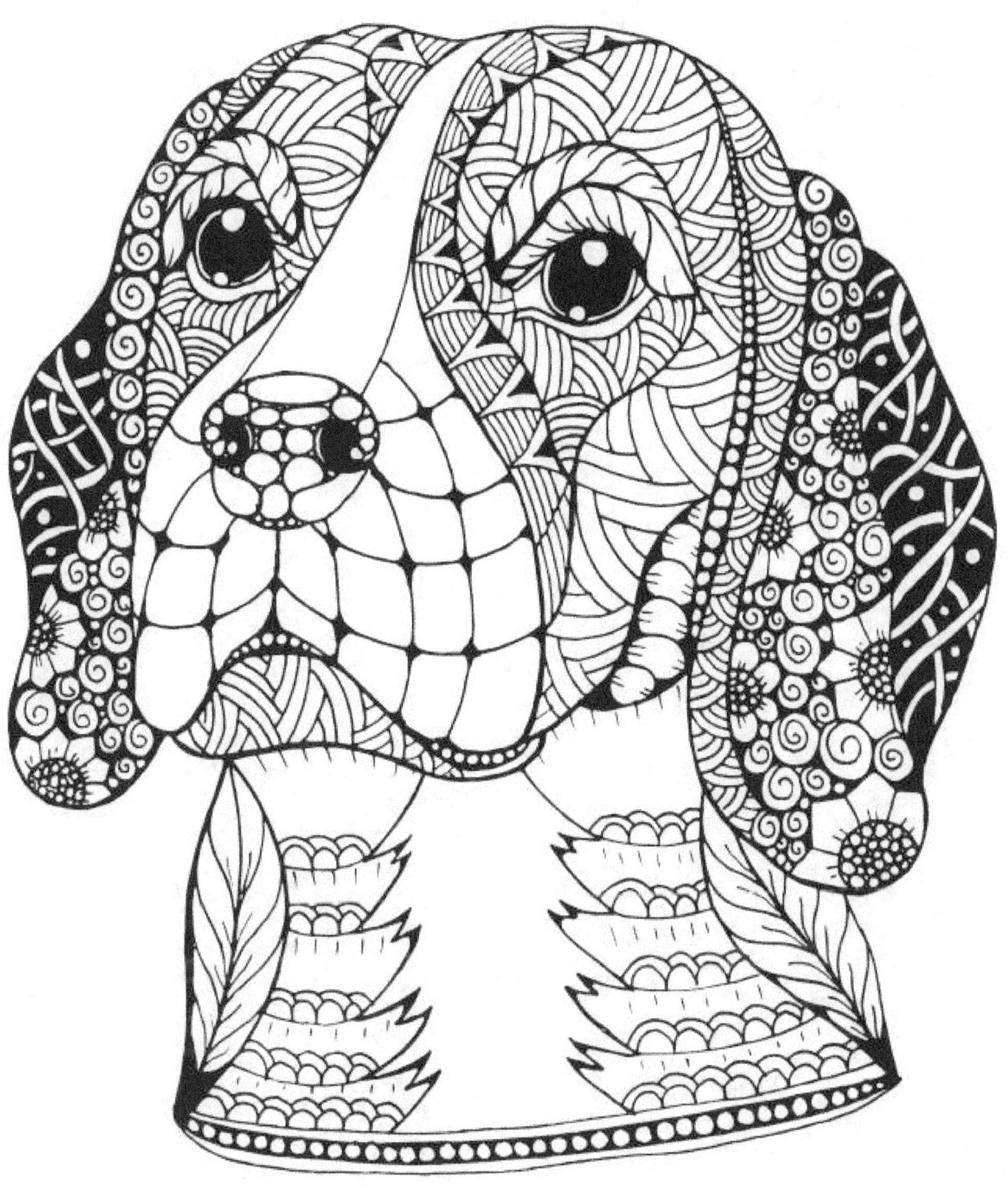

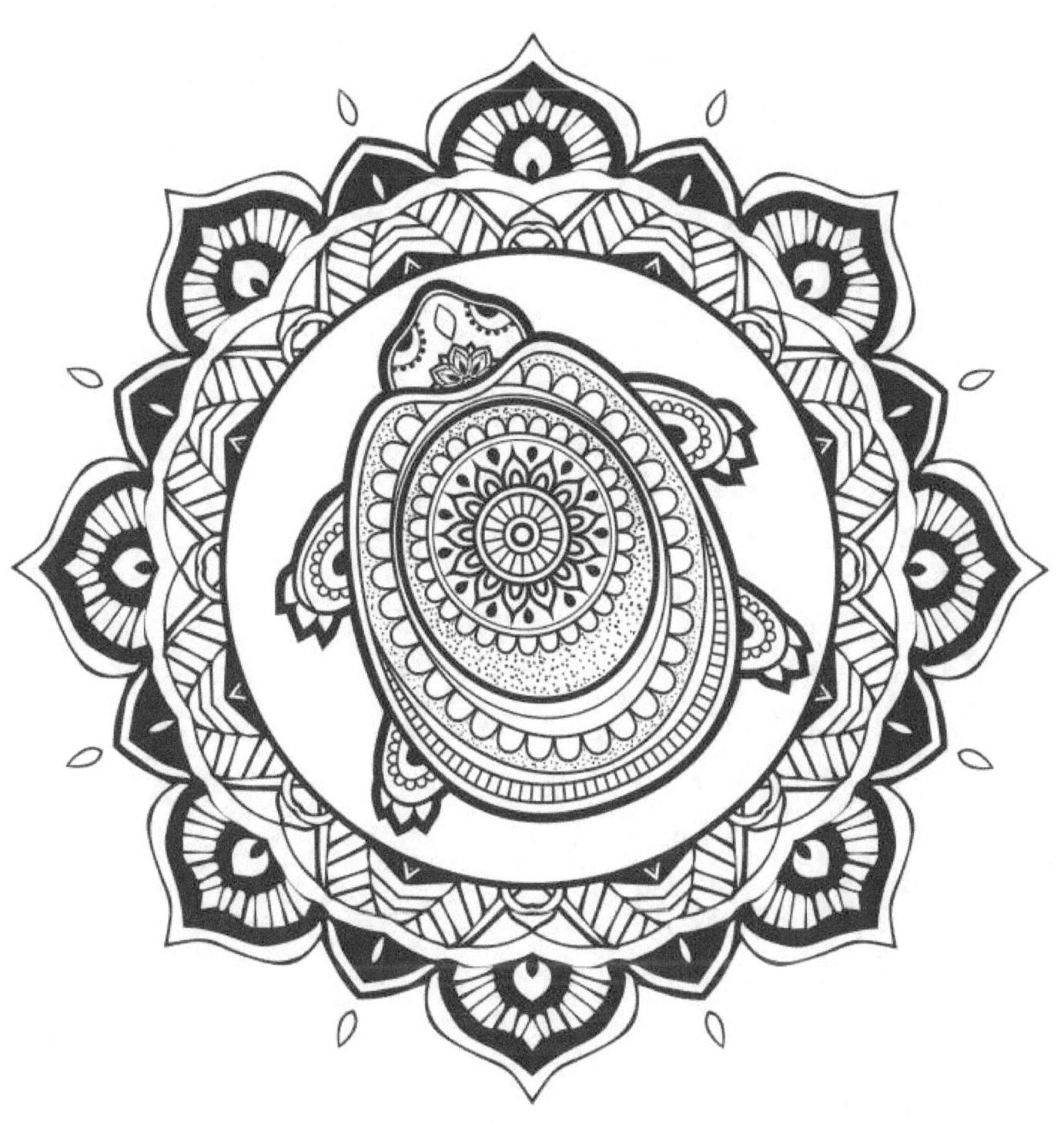

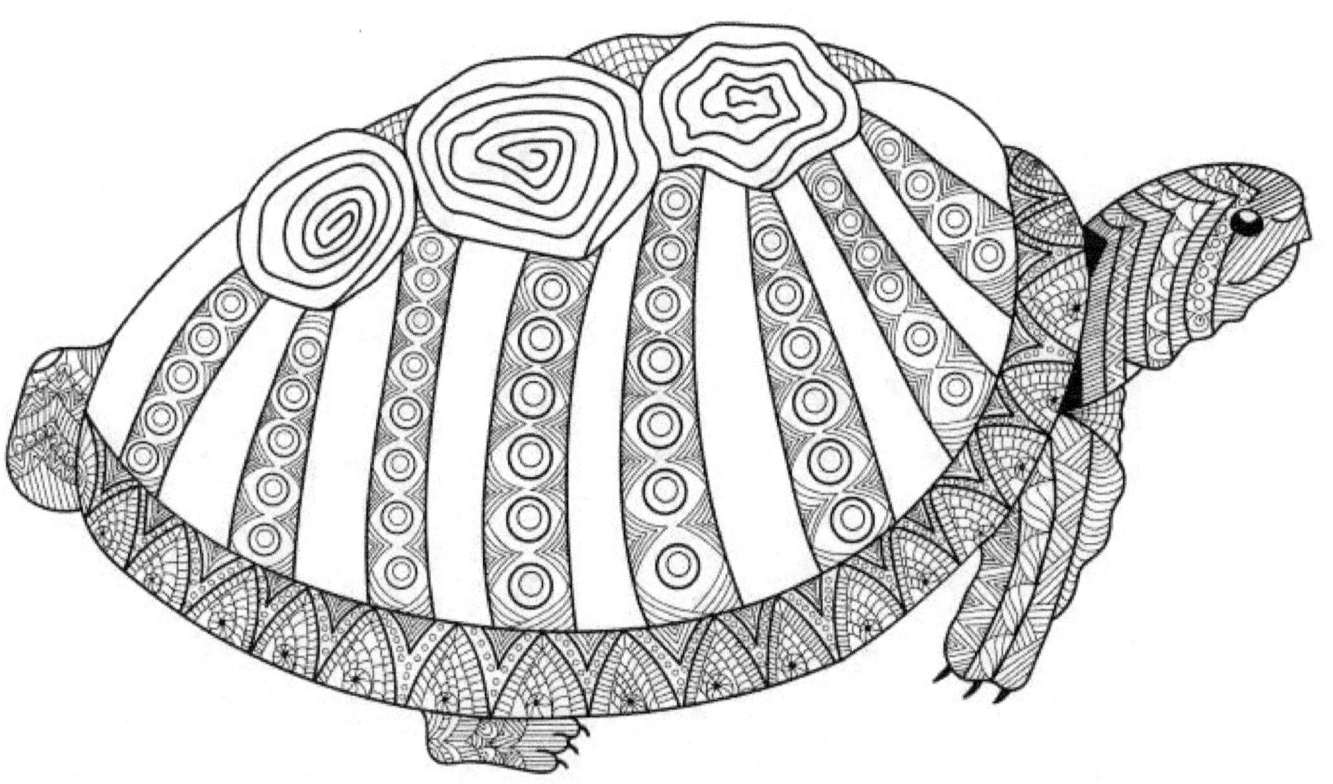

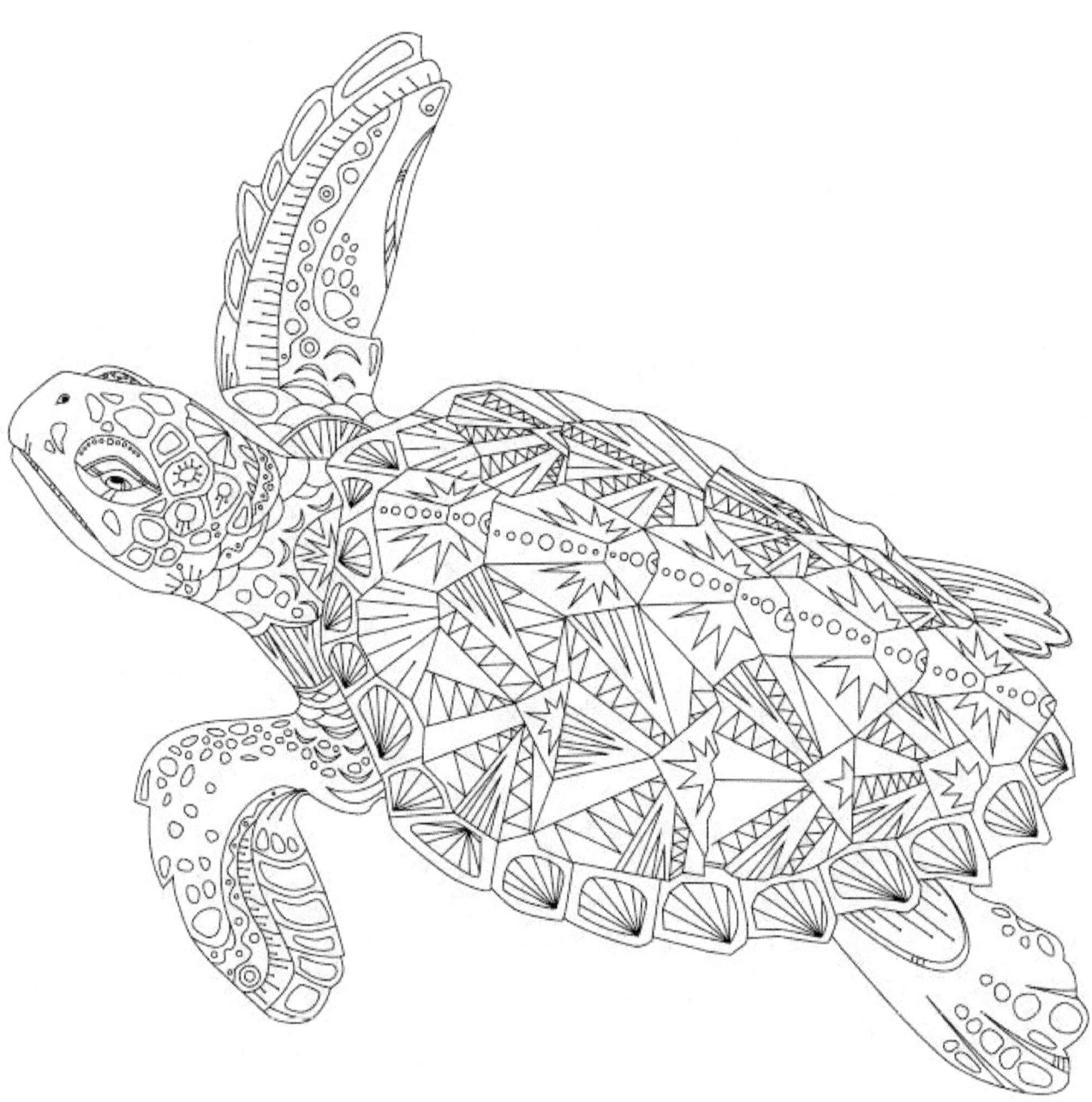

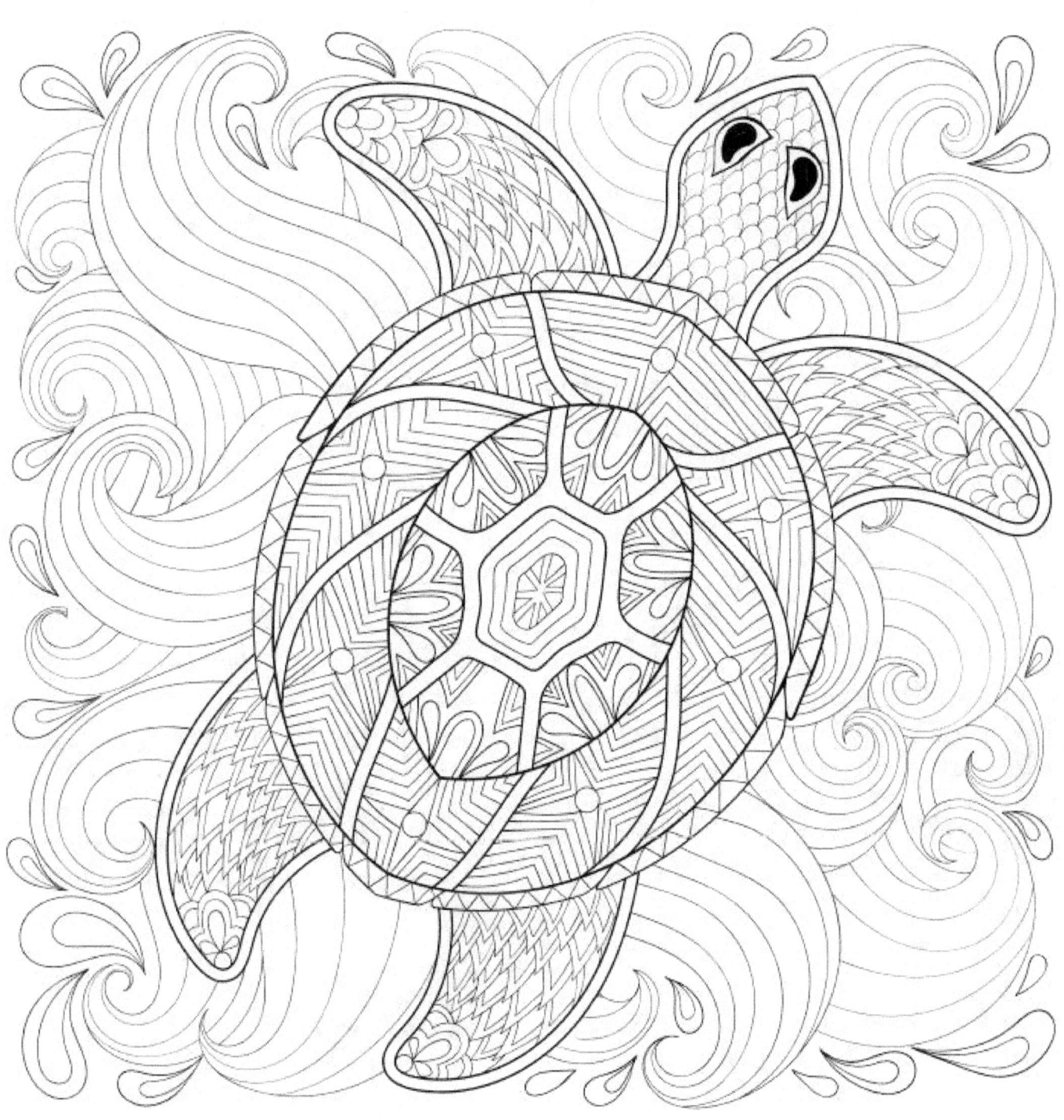

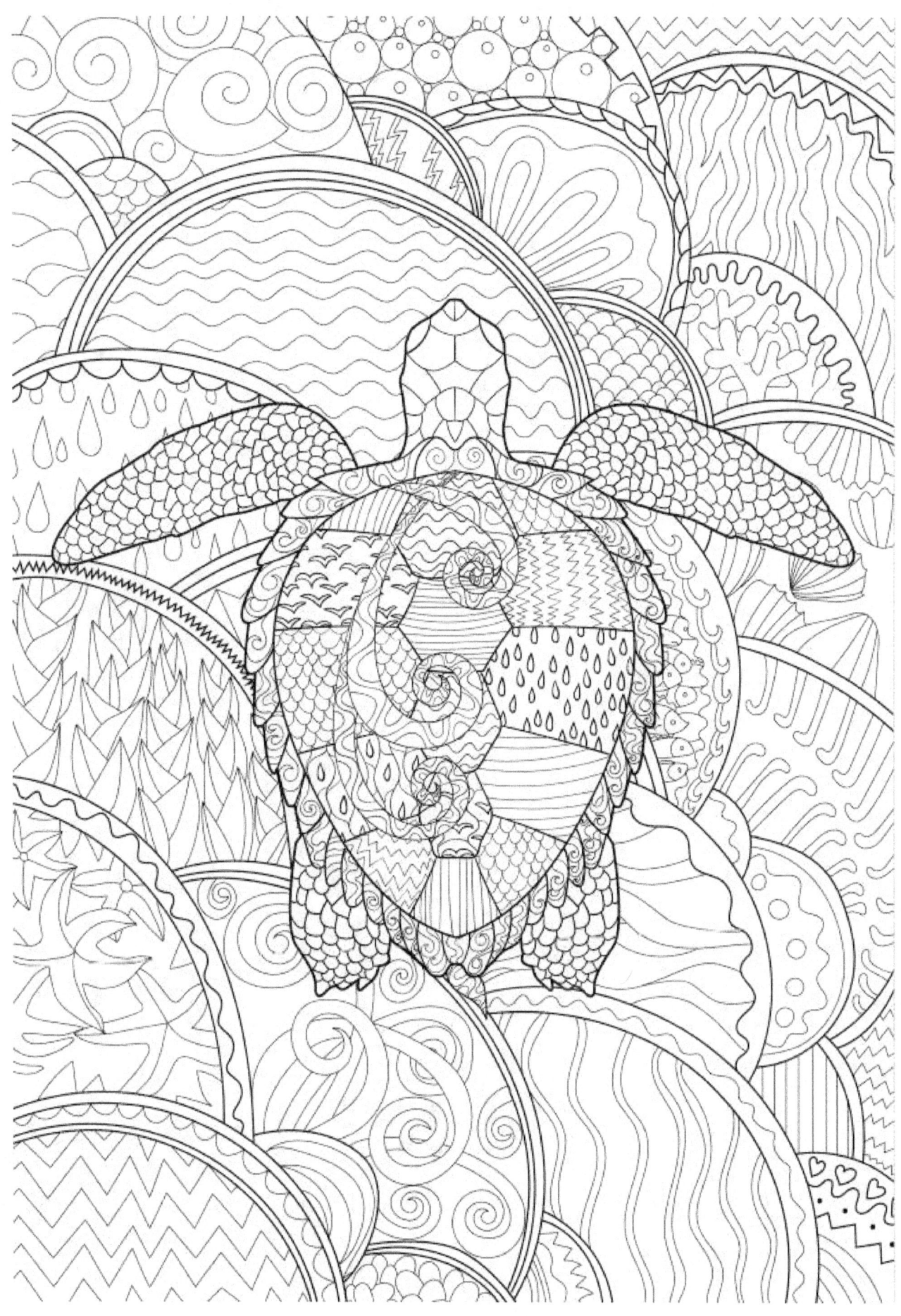

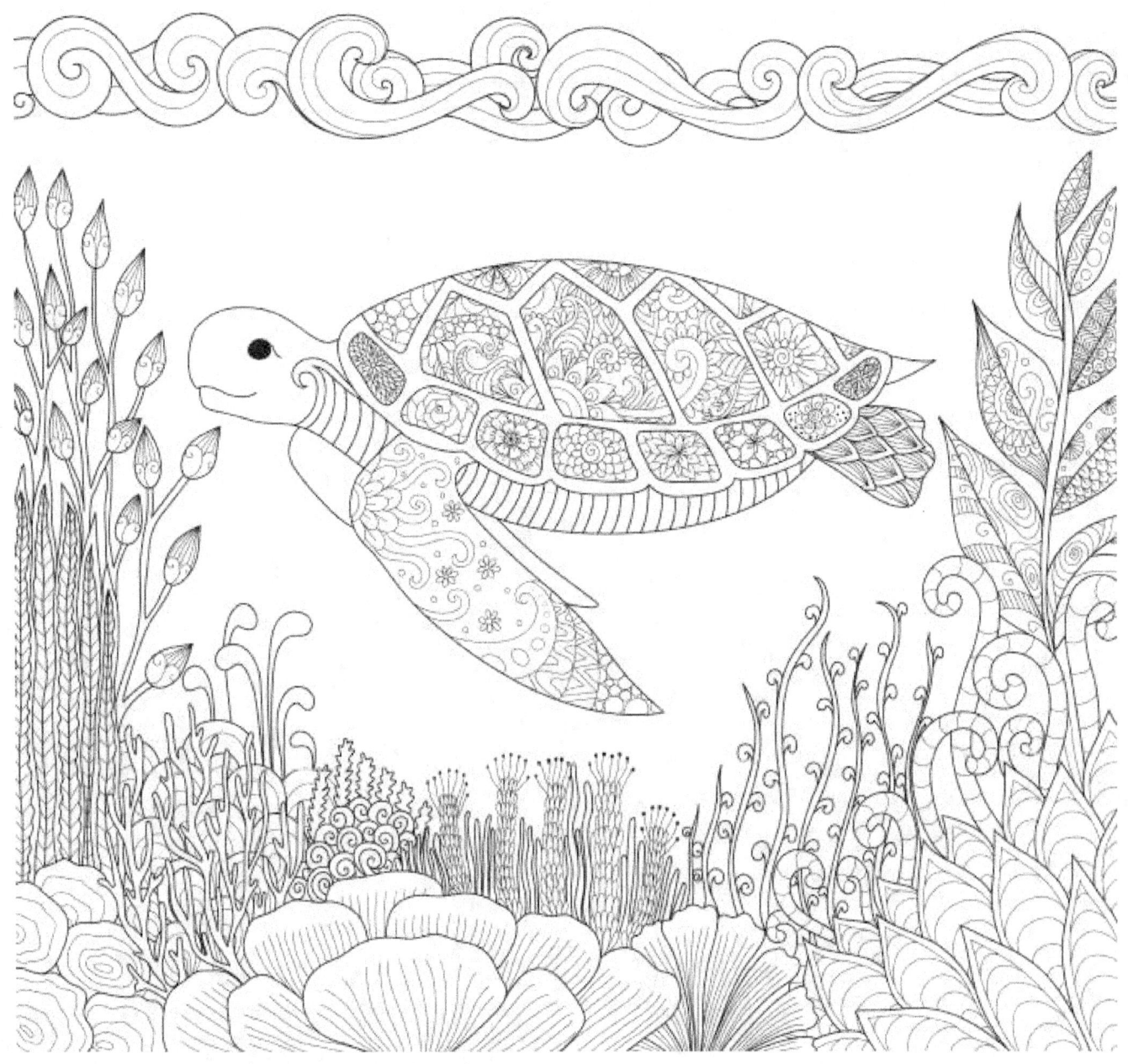

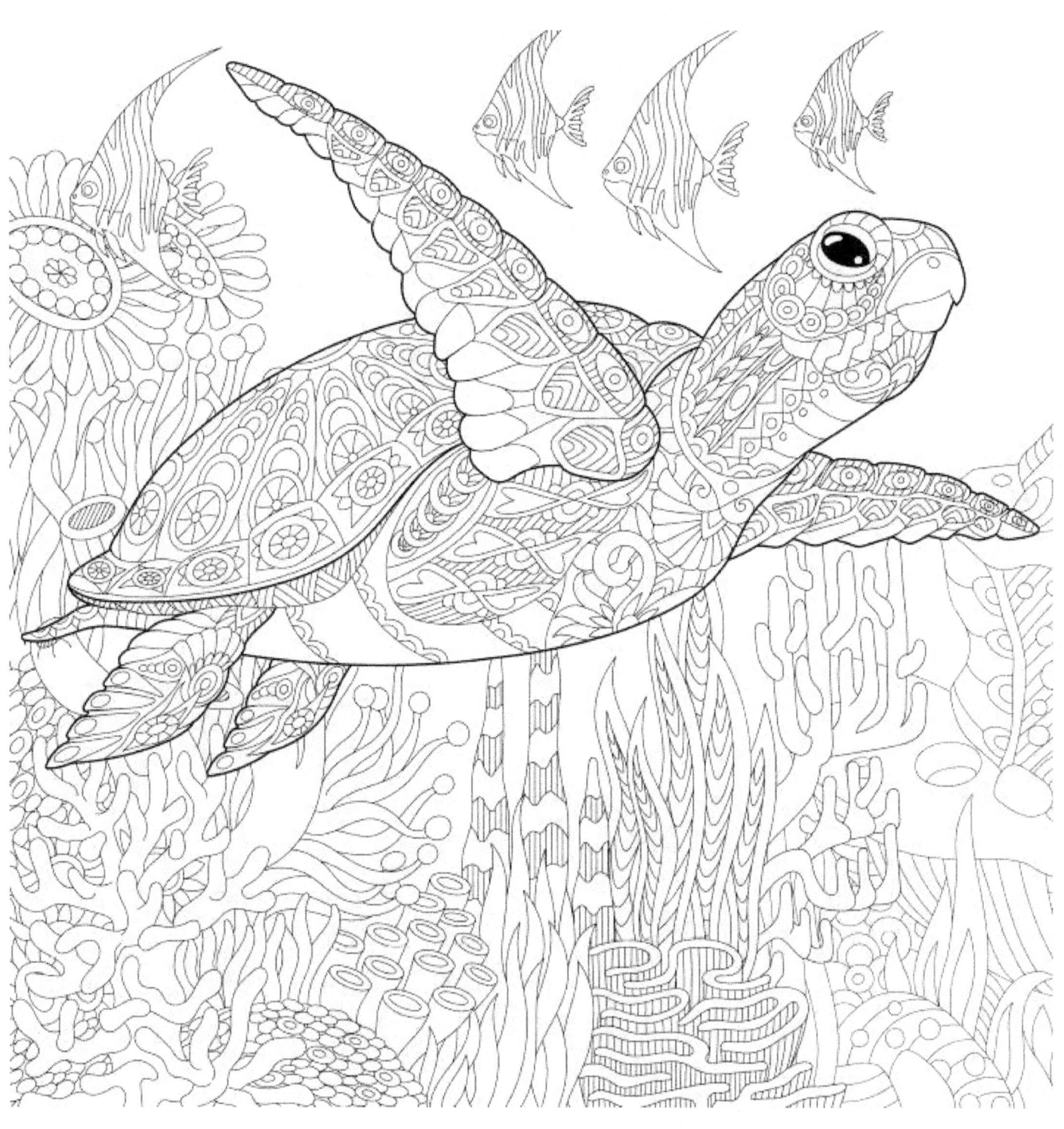

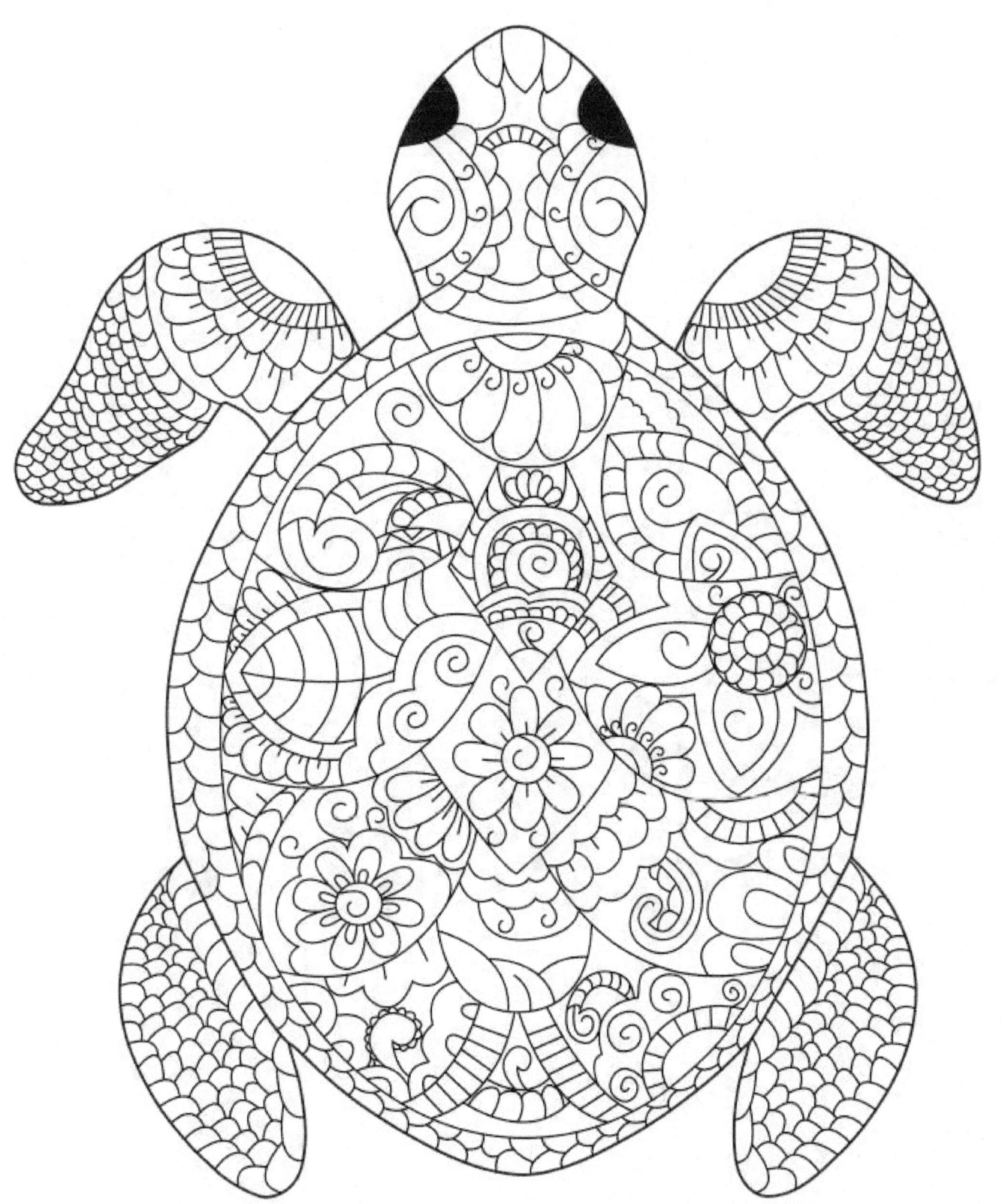

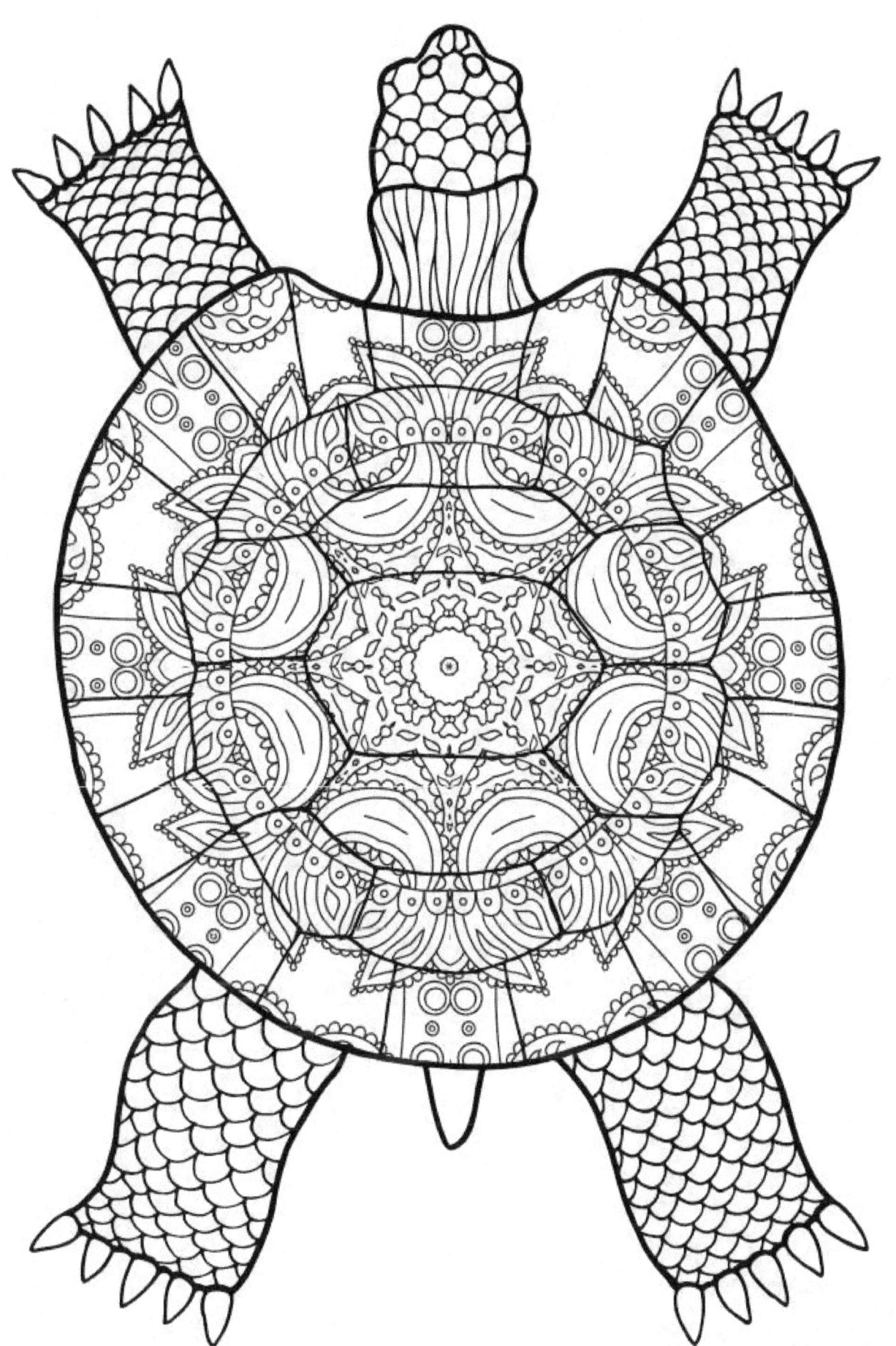

www.ingramcontent.com/pod-product-compliance
Lightning Source LLC
Chambersburg PA
CBHW081215170526
45165CB00009B/2829